Still Waiting for the Jubilee: Pragmatic Solutions for the Third World Debt Crisis

DAVID MALIN ROODMAN

Jane Peterson, *Editor*

WORLDWATCH PAPER 155

April 2001

THE WORLDWATCH INSTITUTE is an independent, nonprofit environmental research organization in Washington, DC. Its mission is to foster a sustainable society in which human needs are met in ways that do not threaten the health of the natural environment or future generations. To this end, the Institute conducts interdisciplinary research on emerging global issues, the results of which are published and disseminated to decision-makers and the media.

FINANCIAL SUPPORT for the Institute is provided by the Compton Foundation, the Geraldine R. Dodge Foundation, the Ford Foundation, the Richard & Rhoda Goldman Fund, the William and Flora Hewlett Foundation, W. Alton Jones Foundation, Charles Stewart Mott Foundation, the Curtis and Edith Munson Foundation, David and Lucile Packard Foundation, John D. and Catherine T. MacArthur Foundation, Summit Foundation, Turner Foundation, U.N. Population Fund, Wallace Genetic Foundation, Wallace Global Fund, Weeden Foundation, and the Winslow Foundation. The Institute also receives financial support from its Council of Sponsors members—Tom and Cathy Crain, James and Deanna Dehlsen, Roger and Vicki Sant, Robert Wallace and Raisa Scriabine, and Eckart Wintzen—and from the many other friends of Worldwatch.

THE WORLDWATCH PAPERS provide in-depth, quantitative and qualitative analysis of the major issues affecting prospects for a sustainable society. The Papers are written by members of the Worldwatch Institute research staff and reviewed by experts in the field. Regularly published in five languages, they have been used as concise and authoritative references by governments, nongovernmental organizations, and educational institutions worldwide. For a partial list of available Papers, see back pages.

The views expressed are those of the author and do not necessarily represent those of the Worldwatch Institute; of its directors, officers, or staff; or of its funding organizations.

Table of Contents

ACKNOWLEDGMENTS: I thank Cheryl Goodman, Rob Mills, Joan Nelson, Kunibert Raffer, Bruce Rich, Christian Suter, and Carol Welch for reviewing early drafts of this paper or the *State of the World* chapter from which it grew. I am greatly indebted (the metaphor will not be denied) to my colleagues Hilary French, Brian Halweil, Michael Renner, and Payal Sampat for their reviews. Thanks also to intern Bryan Mignone for his capable assistance during the summer of 2000, to Art Director Liz Doherty for turning the manuscript into a Paper with her usual competence, and to Denise Warden for shepherding us through the process. And I thank Jane Peterson, editor and friend.

To my wife Hoangmai Pham I owe an unpayable debt, for it is she who lost most in my struggle to be writer, father, and husband all at once. Last, I thank my little son Benjamin, as my father once thanked me, for making sure I got up early every morning to write. To him I dedicate this work.

DAVID MALIN ROODMAN is a Senior Researcher at the Worldwatch Institute, where he writes about the economics and political economy of sustainable development. Mr. Roodman graduated from Harvard College with a degree in theoretical mathematics. His book *The Natural Wealth of Nations: Harnessing the Market for the Environment* appeared in 1998 and argued that overhauls of government taxation and spending policies are needed to make economic development environmentally sustainable. During academic year 1998–99, Mr. Roodman took leave from the Worldwatch Institute to take a Fulbright Scholarship in Vietnam. He now works part-time in order to care for his son.

Introduction

Imagine the distress of Africa, and the Democratic Republic of Congo is the sort of place that comes to mind. Following nearly a century of traumatic subjugation by Belgium, this European-designed nation eventually won independence, in 1960, and sank into violence within a week. After five years of conflict, a man named Mobutu took power by force with the help of the U.S. Central Intelligence Agency and began a rapacious, 31-year reign.[1]

Though Mobutu skillfully cloaked his rule in the language of African nationalism—by giving his nation the supposedly more authentic name of "Zaire," for example—the dynamics of colonialism still held sway. He gave foreign companies access to Zaire's vast natural wealth, which included an estimated quarter of the world's copper and half its cobalt, and threw his cold war allegiance to the West. In exchange, the dictator won generous support from Western investors and governments, including billions of dollars in bank loans and half of all U.S. aid to black Africa in the late 1970s. From these funds, and from export earnings, he siphoned off a personal fortune of some $4 billion by the mid-1980s—a sum not unduly diminished by the purchase of a dozen estates in Continental Europe and chartered-Concorde shopping trips to Paris. It would be wrong to suggest, however, that Mobutu gave nothing to his country. He imported 500 British double-decker buses, built the world's largest supermarket, and erected a steelworks that one banker said the country needed "like it needs central heating."[2]

The descent into hell began in 1975 when Mobutu,

caught short by a plunge in the price of copper, threatened to default. For the next 15 years, he used his geopolitical leverage to force his creditors to defer his debt payments—or to cover them with new loans. He then essentially defaulted on the World Bank and the International Monetary Fund (IMF). Meanwhile, Zaire entered a brutal economic slide. By the mid-1980s, the swollen bellies of the hungry became a common sight. A Belgian volunteer reported seeing "a little girl eating grass and another one who was eating the waste from the brewery....She told me she hadn't eaten for three days."[3]

Today, Mobutu is deposed and dead, but his legacies live on. His family holds his fortune, and his country holds his $12 billion debt. In a nation with an annual income of $110 per capita, each resident theoretically owes foreign creditors $236.[4]

Zaire's disastrous involvement with foreign borrowing is one of the worst (and earliest) cases of its kind in the postcolonial era. It represents, if in caricature, the debt troubles that dozens of other poor countries have run into in recent decades. Currently, to use the World Bank's measuring sticks, some 47 nations are very poor—having a gross national product (GNP) of less than $855 per person—and heavily indebted, with their governments owing foreigners the equivalent of at least 18 months of export earnings. All but 10 of the 47 are in Africa. (See Map.) For most people in these nations, life is hard. Civil wars, coups d'état, corruption, AIDS, famine, illiteracy are all relatively common. And almost no one thinks these countries can repay more than a small fraction of their foreign debts, which now total some $422 billion, or $380 per resident.[5]

The debt crisis in low-income nations—it is commonly called a crisis, though it is actually a slowly developing, chronic syndrome—is one of two major strains of debt trouble that have struck the developing world since the 1970s. The first, which broke out suddenly in 1982, mainly involved "middle-income" countries, such as Turkey, Mexico, and most South American nations, as well as the commercial banks they borrowed from (though "low-income" countries were not completely immune). It largely spent

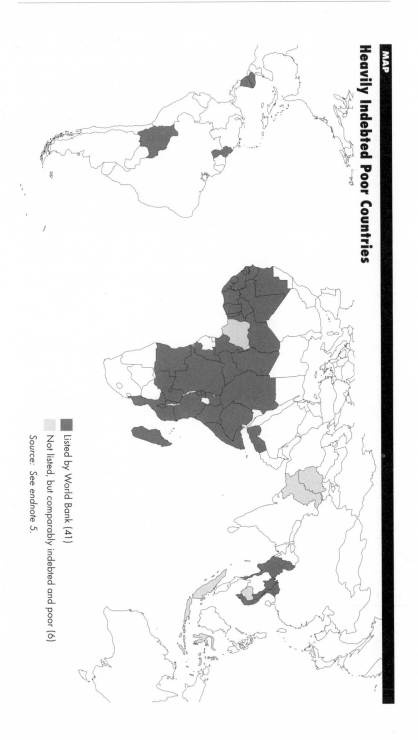

MAP

Heavily Indebted Poor Countries

■ Listed by World Bank (41)

▨ Not listed, but comparably indebted and poor (6)

Source: See endnote 5.

itself in the early 1990s as banks and borrowing governments finally struck compromises on repayment.

The second strain spread gradually in low-income
nations—and has worsened to this day. It is different because
low-income countries, regarded as risky investments by
commercial bankers, have mainly attracted *official* lenders:
aid agencies, "multilateral" lenders such as the World Bank
and the IMF, and export credit agencies (ECAs, which subsi-
dize a country's exporters with cheap credit for their cus-
tomers). While commercial lenders followed the classic
manic-depressive cycles of private finance, first overrunning
countries in their eagerness to lend, then retreating en
masse, official lenders stayed on a more even keel.

For all their steadiness, though, official lenders also have
run aground in the poorest nations, and in a way that is
undermining the worldwide .fight for sustainable development. Hundreds of billions of dollars of official loans have
disappeared into corruption, capital flight, weapons buying,
white elephants, and projects that worked better on paper
than in practice. And now the need to service debts has cut
into government budgets for roads, environmental protection, primary education, and basic healthcare. Indeed, many
low-income debtors spent more servicing debts to the
world's richest nations in the late 1990s than giving social
services to their own impoverished citizens. Meanwhile, private investors and local entrepreneurs—the proverbial haters
of uncertainty—have been discouraged by doubts about
what debtor governments, cornered by their creditors, will
do next. Will they raise tariffs on exports? Or print money,
thereby feeding inflation?[6]

Because debt trouble set in gradually in low-income
countries, no one can point to a particular child dying in
Mozambique from tetanus or to a particular plot of forest
cleared by a poor farmer in Honduras and say with confidence, "Debt caused that." But the experience of middle-
income countries, where debt crisis developed with a
suddenness that spotlighted the link between cause and
effect, offers a vivid picture of its impact. In Mexico, wages

halved between 1982 and 1988. In the Philippines, a million or more desperate peasants moved into the hills, where they cleared erodible slopes of protective trees and farmed to survive. And in southeastern Brazil, immunization cutbacks opened the way for a measles epidemic that killed thousands of babies in 1984.[7]

The debt crisis in the poorest nations thus confronts the world with a dilemma. Critics on one side of the issue point to the theft and waste and ask why taxpayers in rich countries should let incompetent or unaccountable governments off the hook. Debt is a promise to pay, and a promise is a moral obligation. But critics on the other side, represented most effectively by the international Jubilee 2000 coalition of churches and nongovernmental organizations (NGOs), decry the "chains of debt" that enslave the world's poorest nations to the richest ones and, they submit, choke off government spending for immunizing poor children or teaching them how to read.

In 1999, the leaders of the seven leading industrial nations (the G–7) announced their latest response to the debt crisis, the enhanced Debt Initiative for Heavily Indebted Poor Countries (HIPCs). It is easily the most far-reaching debt reduction offer yet, and a sign of the power of Jubilee 2000. The HIPC initiative aims to cut the $205 billion debt of 41 qualifying nations by some 45 percent within perhaps five years. (Six comparably poor and indebted countries are not listed for various reasons.) Additionally, Italy, the United States, and the United Kingdom, among others, have promised to write off all their loans to "the HIPC 41," which could bring the total reduction to 55 percent.[8]

With the debt reduction initiatives, official creditors have taken an important step toward resolving the current debt troubles, and with another big push from the likes of Jubilee 2000, they might go far enough to succeed. However, the initiatives only attack the symptoms of debt crisis. Largely designed by and for creditors, they do little to highlight, much less address, the underlying causes. As a result, they will almost certainly invite fresh crises in the poorest nations. Rich governments have made important financial contributions to the development of poor nations: they have stamped out smallpox, funded family planning programs that have dramatically slowed population growth, and built rural roads and schools. But as long as lending and borrowing occur in ways that invite trouble, loans from foreign governments will probably do as much harm as good.[9]

Several major problems lie at the heart of the debt crisis. All reflect hard economic and political realities. Rich countries restrict imports of crops and clothing and other exports of poor countries, effectively demanding loan repayment while refusing the goods offered as payment. Official agencies often lend to poor countries for reasons that have little to do with aiding their development and assuring their ability to repay loans, and everything to do with winning geopolitical allegiances—or sales for Lockheed Martin and Caterpillar. Loans proffered with more genuine intentions of aiding the borrower run into another problem: they are supposed to be repaid regardless of results, even though failure is to be expected in the difficult business of development. Finally, both the agencies that lend and the ones that borrow are often insulated from the consequences of their actions. This insularity gives free play to bureaucratic tendencies toward arrogance, over-optimism, the pursuit of growth in lending and borrowing for its own sake, and even corruption.

Stating each problem so starkly evokes solutions that are simple in theory. Creditor countries need to buy more goods from debtors. ECAs and other agencies need to put enhancing the borrower's ability to service debt before geopolitics and domestic politics. An international bankruptcy process is needed to make loan write-offs routine and require lenders to bear some costs of failure. And so on.

In practice, however, reform is a challenge as complex as it is vital. Powerful business lobbies, for example, protect ECAs and import barriers; it will take an equally organized political campaign to overcome them. And if official lenders become *too* accountable—too afraid of failure—then they could fall prey to the very herd mentality that once provoked a debt crisis in middle-income nations. The project of reform must proceed with realism to stand a chance of serving, rather than undermining, sustainable development in the poorest nations. If they thrive, the rest of the world can only benefit.

Repeating History

> Progress, far from consisting in change, depends on retentiveness....Those who cannot remember the past are condemned to repeat it.
>
> —George Santayana, *Life of Reason,* 1905–06[10]

> There can be few fields of human endeavor in which history counts for so little as in the world of finance. Past experience, to the extent that it is part of memory at all, is dismissed as the primitive refuge of those who do not have the insight to appreciate the incredible wonders of the present.
>
> —John Kenneth Galbraith, *A Short History of Financial Euphoria,* 1993[11]

These days, the future rushes at us so fast as to make the past seem irrelevant; and to be sure, many of today's experiences are unprecedented in human history. The current debt crisis, however, is not one of them. In fact, the history of international lending repeats itself with remarkable regularity, which suggests that in the world of international finance, people have done a poor job of learning from the past. At the same time, this cyclicity means that there is much experience to learn from as the world tries to do better next time.

Debt, like the wheel, is a useful invention whose origins are lost to history. Unlucky Sumerians may have run up the earliest known debts, recording them by etching lines in clay tablets. Perhaps they were farmers asking their lord's forbearance on taxes, which were payable in bags of grain. Whatever the precise meaning of these markings, they reveal the essence of debt, which has survived unchanged through the bewildering innovations of modern finance: debt is a promise to pay. And *credit* is the acceptance of such a promise.[12]

Governments have long been major, if not dominant, users of credit. To banks and bond investors, governments seem the safest bets around. During the late-twentieth-century international lending boom, Citibank president Walter Wriston expressed the faith in public borrowers when he famously declared that countries "don't go out of business." And for governments, borrowing is tempting because it offers a means of spending without taxing—at least until the loans come due. In the early 1800s, for instance, governments learned to tap newly invented bond markets to build canals or railroads, promising their investors the full faith and credit of the rising industrial powerhouse of Pennsylvania, say, or the sovereign nation of Brazil.[13]

As the Western world has changed, so have the reasons that governments borrow. Before the Industrial Revolution, rulers took out loans mainly to support courtly extravagances or make war. In the early 14th century, for instance, King Edward III of England borrowed heavily from the leading banks of the day, which operated out of Florence, to fund his side of the Hundred Years' War against France. (He then defaulted.) With industrialization came an important new motivation for government borrowing: the pursuit of "economic development." This rationale was best articulated in the early 1800s by Frenchman Claude-Henri Saint-Simon and his disciples. In awe of science and technology, the Saint-Simonians envisioned a utopia in which reason had transformed not only production but government, in which technocrats free from bias and political pressure would finance and manage economic development according to scientific principles. The Saint-Simonians' offspring include socialism, Marxism, the World Bank, and the IMF—and faith in lending for development wherever it is expressed.[14]

The Saint-Simonians were off the mark in their unbridled optimism, but not in their appreciation of the role that lending was assuming in economic life. In the 1800s, international lending became a central artery of capitalism and imperialism, and increasingly facilitated the gains and the depredations of the industrial age. Within Europe and the Americas, cross-border lending fostered economic development that eventually lifted millions of people out of poverty. Countries that began industrializing earliest financed canals and railroads and factories in places that began industrializing later, such as the United States and the Italian peninsula. Between 1816 and 1913, net capital exports from Great Britain, the dominant international lender of the era, climbed from some $80 million a year (in dollars of the day) to more than $1.1 billion.[15]

One measure of the economic effectiveness of foreign lending is that, since 1820, it has profited investors who diversified and persevered—more so than lending at home. Foreign bonds, with their higher interest rates to reflect risk, were honored often enough to cover losses. But by the same token, international lending facilitated the worst abuses of capitalism—the Central American banana plantations or South African gold mines or American cigar factories that exploited workers in slave or near-slave conditions.[16]

If international lending has been a handmaiden to industrialism, it has been an unruly one. From the boom and bust in tulip bulbs, which sent Holland into an economic depression in the 1630s, to the Asian crisis of 1997, the volatility of financial markets has frequently exacted a harsh economic price. In a review of international lending since 1820, Swiss sociologist Christian Suter identified four major waves of international borrowing, occurring roughly every 50 years. (See Figure 1.) Each terminated with an outbreak of "debt service incapacity"—a widespread inability to keep up with interest and principal payments—causing banks and bond investors to beat a hasty retreat. The world's greatest economic setbacks, including those in the 1870s, 1930s, and 1980s, all began this way.[17]

These cyclical shifts of capital into and out of developing countries are not fully understood. But human psychology is

FIGURE 1

Number of Countries Not Servicing All Their Foreign Debts, 1820–1999

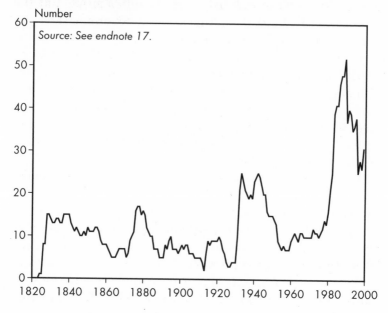

clearly at work in the wildness of the swings. Ignorant of the future, investors often look to each other for cues, and so move in herds, through euphoria and panic. In a few years in the 1870s, for example, net capital exports from Great Britain zoomed from $250 million to $500 million a year and then crashed to $100 million after foreign governments started defaulting.[18]

Then, as now, investors drew confidence from various rationales during the upswings, many of which contained truth—Brazil, for example, with its rich resources, industrious immigrants, and modern government, was the next United States. But excessive investor enthusiasm made fertile ground for waste and fraud—and, eventually, default. In the 1920s, for instance, Colombia's federal government borrowed $150 million ($1.4 billion in 2000 dollars) to drill a rail link under a 3,000-meter (9,000-foot) mountain range in order to con-

nect two valleys that already had good transportation con-
nection via the sea. At the same time, local authorities built a
road over the mountains. In such cases, the cascade of new
bonds would temporarily cover payments on the old ones
(since the projects could not). But once one country defaulted, creditors would lose confidence and stop lending to other
countries as well, and the crisis would expand, a pattern that
has sporadically affected commercial lending ever since.[19]

Another source of fragility in international lending
would then become apparent: the ambiguous legal relationship between lenders and borrowers. It is hard for a lender to
enforce the law of contracts against a debtor when the debtor
is the law—harder still when the debtor is a foreign government, and there is *no* clearly applicable law. As S.C. Gwynne,
a former U.S. bank loan officer, has put it, "international
banks cannot 'collect' a power plant in Thailand or a hospi-
tal in Dubai, or even a Caterpillar tractor in the jungles of
Kalimantan. They cannot 'tag' a banana crop in the
Philippines, or grab the copper as it comes out of the mine."[20]

Defaults naturally angered the creditors; but in the end,
they always had to come to terms with their losses, however
reluctantly. After several U.S. states defaulted in the 1830s, one
prominent English bond investor excoriated the United States
as "a nation with whom no contract can be made, because
none will be kept; unstable in the very foundations of social
life, deficient in the elements of good faith." Such indignation
is understandable, but misses the reality that sharing losses is
the companion of lending overshoot. Bankruptcy codes in
most nations, honed over centuries, recognize that letting a
bankrupt survive to do business another day is often in the
interest of all concerned. They also recognize that forcing
overeager lenders to take a loss teaches a healthy prudence. The
hole in international law where a bankruptcy code belongs has
not made international compromise less necessary. But it has
forced creditors and debtors to negotiate in ad hoc fashion, to
the detriment of all concerned, especially debtors. Between
1820 and 1975, a grueling nine years elapsed on average
between outbreak of a crisis and its resolution.[21]

Debtors, too, have usually had to swallow their anger. Only on rare occasions has a new government come to power and declared the debts of its predecessor to be legally "odious." In 1898, the United States forcibly took over the Spanish colony of Cuba, but refused to assume its debts. The former colonial government had used the money to put down an independence movement, even interring suspects in concentration camps. Loans used against the people, the United States asserted, should not be the responsibility of the people. In the early 1920s, a new government in Costa Rica refuted foreign debts contracted by the just-deposed dictator, Federico Tinoco Granados. U.S. Chief Justice and former President William Howard Taft sat as arbitrator in the dispute and sided firmly with Costa Rica. He pointed out that the bank knew that Tinoco would squirrel away the money for personal use. A few such exceptions aside, however, only great powers, or nations exiting the capitalist financial system, such as China and Russia after their communist revolutions, have dared repudiate their obligations. Most governments opted to compromise with creditors over old loans, no matter how unfair the burden, in order to get new ones.[22]

Remarkably, the same nations often held the roles of debtor or creditor from crisis to crisis. Since 1820, Latin American and East European nations have frequently run into debt trouble. (See Table 1.) (Most of Africa was off the lending map until the 1960s.) Worldwide, at least three quarters of the countries that avoided debt problems in any of four major lending periods between 1820 and 1979 did so in the next one as well. The same persistence held among countries that *did* run into trouble, except that the Great Depression had many one-time defaulters. This pattern holds even when comparing 1820–1929 with 1980–86, with 64 percent of problem debtors in the years between Napoleon and Hitler resurfacing to haunt lenders in the era of Reagan and Thatcher. Meanwhile, a handful of countries—Britain, France, Germany, the United States, and Japan—accounted for most overlending.[23]

This regularity suggests that the tendency to overborrow

TABLE 1

International Debt Crises since 1820

Period	Selected Major Debtors	Selected Major Creditors	Approximate Debt with Payment Problems (billion 2000 $)
1826–30	Greece, Latin America, Spain	British bond investors	3
1840–45	Mexico, Portugal, Spain, nine U.S. states	British and French bond investors	6
1875–82	Egypt, Greece, Latin America, Ottoman Empire,[1] Spain, Tunisia, 10 southern U.S. states	British bond investors; German banks; French government	40
1890–1900	Greece, Latin America, Portugal, Serbia	German and British bond investors; Barings Bank	20
1911–18	Bulgaria, Mexico, Ottoman Empire,[1] Russia[2]	French bond investors	200
1931–40	China, France, Germany, Greece, Hungary, Latin America, Poland, Turkey, United Kingdom, Yugoslavia	World War I victors (owed by Germany); U.S. government (owed by other victors); Western bond investors	300
1982–	Latin America, Philippines, Poland, Africa, Turkey, Yugoslavia	French, West German, Japanese, U.K., U.S. banks; G–7 governments; IMF, World Bank	400

[1] Predecessor to modern Turkey. [2] Accounted for as much as 85 percent of defaulted amount in this period.
Source: See endnote 23.

or overlend emerges from deep within a nation's character and history. One generalization that seems useful is that the most internally divided nations make the most troubled debtors. Almost all Latin American states, as well as the Philippines, inherited from their colonial rulers Spain and Portugal an extreme concentration of wealth in the hands of the few, which has been perpetuated down through the centuries. These powerful elites have generally fought off government efforts to tax them and help those less well off. For leaders of such divided societies, foreign borrowing is tempting as a way to aid one group by, say, financing coal plants to generate jobs and cheap power, without taxing another group—or at least to forestall the day of reckoning.

The current debt crisis stands apart from past ones in that governments have been not only the major borrowers, but major lenders. Nevertheless, its roots are deep. In the recent lending cycle, as in all those before, many loans have been put to good use while others have not. And the awkward drama of overshoot, crisis, and compromise is once again playing itself out on the international stage. The cyclicity suggests that only a serious attempt to learn from history can prevent yet more troubles in the decades ahead.

International Debt Today

Modern international debt troubles are at once a familiar tale and a standout in the annals of finance. The latest lending upswing began in earnest in the late 1960s. It was punctuated by spectacular international crashes in 1982 and 1997, as well as numerous smaller crises, from Zaire's near-default in 1975 to Ecuador's troubles in 1999. Most disturbing for the present, a chronic debt problem has taken shape in the world's poorest nations. The terrain of modern international lending troubles is therefore quite complex, and best approached at first through the numbers.

The cumulative debt of developing and former Eastern

bloc nations has shot upward with barely a pause in recent decades, from $270 billion in 1970 to $2.6 trillion in 1999 (in 2000 dollars). (See Figure 2.) Private investors—mainly commercial banks and bond investors—have led in lending, with a cumulative $1.2 trillion in outstanding long-term loans at the end of 1999. (Less data is available on short-term loans, which are due for repayment within one year.)[24]

Not far behind are official lenders, which generally come in two stripes. "Bilateral" agencies, which belong to individual governments, held $550 billion in debts at the end of 1999. Next, the jointly funded multilateral lenders, including the World Bank, the IMF, and regional development banks in Africa, Asia, Europe, and Latin America, were owed $440 billion. Official lenders can also be categorized by purpose: export credit agencies, all of which are bilateral, exist to stimulate a nation's exports of wheat or weapons or con-

FIGURE 2

Cumulative Foreign Debt of Developing and Former Eastern Bloc Nations, 1970–99

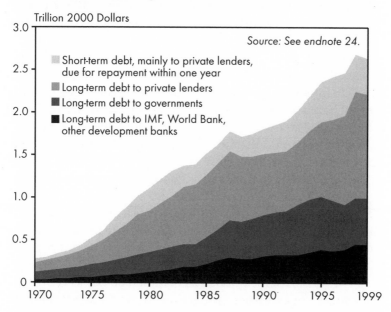

Trillion 2000 Dollars

Source: See endnote 24.

Short-term debt, mainly to private lenders, due for repayment within one year
Long-term debt to private lenders
Long-term debt to governments
Long-term debt to IMF, World Bank, other development banks

struction services by lending the purchase amounts to foreigners, or by guaranteeing repayment of commercial loans
for the same purpose. They held $390 billion of the debt of
developing and former Eastern bloc nations. And aid agencies, both bilateral and multilateral, aim to help poor countries develop.[25]

On the borrowing side, official bodies dominate. At the
end of 1999, governments owed or guaranteed fully 81 percent of the outstanding foreign debt, in the latter case
promising to repay if a domestic borrower, such as an elec-
tric utility, does not.[26]

In the ideal, governments and government-backed borrowers would have invested all this money wisely—in everything from public railroads to business expansion to
education—in order to earn enough foreign exchange to
repay the loans. In practice, however, countries often wasted
substantial sums through corruption, arms buying, and projects that had as much to do with prestige and politics as economics, such as expensive dams. All these uses weakened
borrowers' ability to repay debts. (See "Where Has All the
Money Gone?" below.) To complicate matters, falling prices
for key exports of many developing countries since the
1970s eroded their ability to earn foreign exchange.

The debt crisis that struck in 1982 has been the most
spectacular symptom of these problems. In 1980 and 1981,
U.S. Federal Reserve Chairman Paul Volcker hiked short-term
interest rates to an unheard-of 20 percent in order to fight
inflation. Volcker won his battle, but only after raising interest rates on many outstanding international bank loans and
slowing the global economy. High interest rates and global
recession lit the dry tinder of a decade of excessive lending
and borrowing. In August 1982, the Mexican Minister of
Finance, in the words of a U.S. Treasury Department official,
"showed up at our doorstep and turned his pockets inside
out." Mexico announced that it was close to defaulting on
$80 billion it owed to U.S. and other banks. As in Asia in
1997, the crisis then exploded as commercial banks retreated
from dozens of countries. Altogether, of the $800 billion that

developing and Eastern bloc nations then owed foreigners, about $250 billion became problem debt, meaning that the countries had to defer or cancel promised payments on it during the 1980s.[27]

Yet the crisis of 1982 left surprisingly slight marks on the overall upward trend in debt: it is just discernible in Figure 2 as a tiny dip during 1988. One reason for the deceptively smooth rise is that when debtors have fallen behind on their interest payments in recent decades, creditors have lent more to cover part of the interest and avoid formal default. As a result, many nations emitted cash to the rest of the world even as they went deeper into debt.

Official creditors have moved on a far different track from the commercial lenders who were at the center of the 1982 crisis. The contrast appears most sharply in statistics on "net transfers on lending"—the differences between what countries receive in new loan disbursements each year and what they spend making principal and interest payments on old ones. (See Figure 3.) Net transfers between commercial lenders and their borrowers have swung wildly since 1970. But net transfers from official lenders rose steadily between 1970 and 1981, from $8 billion to $45 billion (in 2000 dollars), then gradually went negative as grace periods expired and bills for interest and principal payments came due. Even the huge IMF and World Bank "bailout packages" for Brazil, Indonesia, South Korea, and other countries since 1997 only sent transfers positive momentarily. As a result, developing and former Eastern bloc nations gave official creditors $40 billion *more* between 1990 and 1999 than they received from those creditors.[28]

The lowest-income countries still received more as a group from official lenders than they paid in the late 1990s—but only barely, and some individual countries received less. (See Figure 4.) Many low-income countries are only maintaining the appearance of fully servicing their debts by borrowing still more—a sure sign that a good share of their debt is unpayable. Today, some 47 nations, labeled here the "Worldwatch 47," are heavily indebted and poor according

FIGURE 3

Net Transfers[1] on Lending into Developing and Former Eastern Bloc Nations, Estimated by Type of Lender, 1970–99

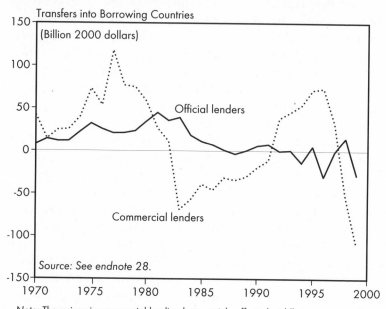

Note: The swings in commercial lending have mainly affected middle-income countries.
[1]Net transfers are disbursements of new loans minus interest and principal payments on old ones.

to criteria set by the World Bank, generally meaning that each has a GNP per capita under $855 a year, and that its government's foreign debts are equivalent to at least 18 months of export earnings.[29]

The Worldwatch 47 include most of Africa, as well as Bolivia, Guyana, Honduras, and Nicaragua; Afghanistan and Pakistan; and Cambodia, Indonesia, Myanmar, and Vietnam. Together, these nations owed $422 billion to foreign creditors at the end of 1999. That is equal to $380 per resident on the debtor side—a substantial sum in such poor countries, but equivalent to only 11 months of Western military spending. Commercial banks held 31 percent of the debt,

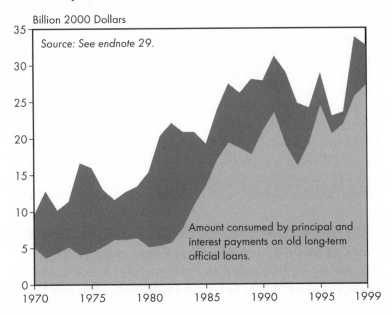

FIGURE 4

Long-term Official Lending to Low-income Developing Countries, 1970–99

Billion 2000 Dollars

Source: See endnote 29.

Amount consumed by principal and interest payments on old long-term official loans.

bilateral creditors 37 percent, and multilaterals 32 percent. (Excluding the fallen giant Indonesia, official creditors dominate even more: bilaterals held 45 percent of the debt and multilaterals 38 percent.) These figures may understate the problem: debt cancellation campaigners at Jubilee 2000 in London have argued that Haiti, Jamaica, Zimbabwe, and some other nations that exceed the World Bank's criteria for "poor" and "heavily indebted" are also deep in debt trouble.[30]

What is beyond debate is that the countries meeting the World Bank criteria are among the most troubled on earth. Thirty-seven of the Worldwatch 47 rank in or just above the U.N. Development Programme's lowest category of human development. This generally means that babies born there can be expected to live 40–50 years, that fewer than half the children and young adults attend school or college, and that barely half the adults can read. Despite all the problems, many of these countries are forced to spend more on foreign debt service than on basic social services. (See Table 2.) In Zambia, the government devoted 40 percent of its national budget to foreign debt payments in 1997 and only 7 percent to basic health and education, clean water, sanitation, family planning, and nutrition combined. The death rate among children there is rising, partly because a third of those under five have not received the vaccines they need, even though they are cheap and effective.[31]

Also beyond debate is that these countries are so deep in debt that most can repay only a fraction of their loans. Today, you can buy commercial IOUs of Benin or Rwanda for about 10 cents on the dollar. Honduras' commercial debt goes for 25 cents on the dollar. Private investors, in other words, do not expect the Worldwatch 47 to repay most of

TABLE 2

Share of Government Spending Covered by Foreign Borrowing and Devoted to Foreign Debt Service and Basic Social Services, Selected Countries, 1996–97[1]

Country	Share Covered by Foreign Borrowing	Share Devoted to Foreign Debt Service	Share Devoted to Basic Social Services
		(percent)	
Belize[2]	8	6	20
Benin[3]	29	11	10
Bolivia[3]	16	10	17
Burkina Faso[3]	20	10	20
Cameroon[4]	36	36	4
El Salvador[2]	47	27	13
Jamaica[2]	14	31	10
Nepal[3]	33	15	14
Nicaragua[2]	14	14	9
Zambia[3]	13	40	7

[1]Basic social services include basic health and education, clean water, sanitation, family planning, and nutrition. [2]Data for 1996. [3]Data for 1997. [4]Data for 1996–97.
Source: See endnote 31.

their debts. Economist Daniel Cohen at the Organisation for Economic Co-operation and Development in Paris has drawn on the experience of middle-income debtors in the 1980s to project how much poor countries will ultimately pay on their loans from both commercial and public lenders. His techniques suggest that the Worldwatch 47 are politically and economically capable of paying back $131 billion, or about 31 percent of their $422 billion in debt. The other $291 billion, this implies, is gone for good.[32]

These stark numbers confront the world with a dilemma. Should official creditors cancel most of their loans to countries in such desperate straits? Or will annulment only reward corruption and dictatorship? The numbers pose the dilemma, but they cannot untangle it. Doing that—assessing how best to end the official debt crisis and prevent its recurrence—requires peering behind the cold numbers. The next three sections present the tragedy in all its dimensions—human and environmental, economic and political. They describe the waste that led to the crisis, and official creditors' failed attempts to end it by lending still more. And they examine how lenders came to be agents and accomplices of the debacle.

Where Has All the Money Gone?

After years of studying our foreign aid program, we have learned that foreign aid is only as good as the recipient government. Foreign aid only reinforces the status quo. It cannot transform an antidemocratic process working against the majority into a participatory government shaped in its interests. Where the recipient government answers only to a narrow economic elite or foreign corporations, our aid not only fails to reach the hungry, it girds the very forces working against them.

—Frances Moore Lappé, Joseph Collins, and Peter Rosset, *World Hunger: Twelve Myths*, 1998[33]

During their annual gathering in 1999, the leaders of the G–7 launched the enhanced Debt Initiative for Heavily Indebted Poor Countries, which set a goal of canceling about 45 percent of the government debt of 41 eligible poor countries. It seemed a generous move, but it was in fact a reconciliation with reality, since most of the debt will probably never be repaid. The reconciliation was only partial at that: economist Cohen estimates that the HIPC 41 can repay roughly $49 billion of their $205 billion debt—far less than they would still owe on paper.[34]

Such big losses provoke a blunt question: Where did all the money go? It is impossible to make a precise accounting. In the electronic age, disbursed loan monies move with the speed of lightning. And many of the people and organizations moving the money cloak their operations in secrecy. Among the Worldwatch 47, the 17 included in Transparency International's (TI's) 2000 corruption survey scored an average of only 2.6 out of 10 (with a lower number indicating more corruption). In addition, the relationship between how loans are used and how easily they are repaid is complex. Some countries, for example, may have put their loans to good use, only to encounter debt trouble as the rising price of oil consumed their foreign exchange. Conversely, others may have wasted much of their borrowings but stayed ahead of their debts through strong economic growth.[35]

On balance, however, the scale of the debt trouble in the poorest nations points to widespread waste, misuse, or failure of development projects. For instance, much of the money borrowed from abroad in the name of the poor headed right back out to foreign bank accounts held by rich compatriots. In Latin America, the rise in public foreign debt during 1976–84 was *roughly matched* by the simultaneous outflow of private capital to banks in New York, the Cayman Islands, or other financial capitals. In Haiti, dictator Baby Doc Duvalier pulled together a private fortune worth $1.5 billion. Worldwide, according to TI's rule of thumb, 10–20 percent of the spending financed by export credit agencies goes to kickbacks.[36]

Borrowers spent billions more on weapons. At best, the tanks and planes were the economic equivalent of Swiss bank accounts: financial sinkholes. At worst, they were tools of repression and impoverishment in the hands of despots. During 1972–82, non-oil-exporting developing countries spent an amount equal to 20 percent of their borrowings on arms from western exporters, according to the Stockholm International Peace Research Institute. Rough estimates indicate that sub-Saharan Africa imported $7 billion in weapons in 1987, and $1 billion in 1997 (the decline being a sign of the end of cold war). These imports fed internal or cross-border wars involving at least 17 African debtor nations, including Angola, Ethiopia, Liberia, and Uganda. In 1999, the Indonesian military, a longtime customer of western lenders and arms manufacturers, used British Hawk fighter jets to back its violent rampage against East Timorese who had voted for independence. As U.N. peacekeeping troops moved in, the country defaulted on $250 million in loans for the Hawks. The British government then swooped in to save the banks since it had guaranteed the loans. In effect, British taxpayers paid for the Hawks used over East Timor.[37]

The evidence of the extent of theft and arms buying seems to imply that the debt crises in low-income countries is a simple matter of despotism run amok. Indeed, few of the Worldwatch 47 had mechanisms to hold governments accountable to the governed, such as a legislature elected through free and fair elections. Their average score on Freedom House's seven-point political rights scale was a high 5.9 in the 1970s and 1980s (indicating a lack of political rights) and 5.1 in the 1990s.[38]

But the truth is more subtle. Following the historical pattern, debt trouble has arisen most in nations that are deeply riven—whether by wealth, as in Latin America, or by ethnicity, as in Africa, where colonial powers stamped a coarse political map over a finer tribal tapestry. In Bolivia in the mid-1980s, the wealthiest fifth of the people earned 15 times as much as the poorest fifth; this societal division led to a "degeneration of politics into...fierce battles of the 'ins' ver-

sus the 'outs'," according to economists Juan Antonio
Morales and Jeffrey D. Sachs. One effect has been "fiscal
indiscipline, since powerful high-income groups veto the
income and wealth taxes that would be needed to finance"
public spending to create jobs or aid the poor. In the 1970s,
Bolivian governments borrowed heavily to expand the public payroll without raising taxes, and thus defer the underlying political conflict between the elites and urban workers.
That made political sense but was consumption from the
point of view of loan repayment, not investment.[39]

Moreover, many authoritarians were genuinely ambitious for their nation's economic development. Unwitting
heirs of Saint-Simon, they took out loans to build their
dreams. In many cases, they used the money well. Indeed,
two big developing-country borrowers—Brazil in the 1970s
and South Korea later—won the imprimatur of "economic
miracle" for their rapid growth in production and exports.
Brazil invested its massive foreign borrowings in dams and
nuclear power, in cement, steel, aircraft, and weapons man-
ufacture, and more. Whatever their environmental and
social merits, some of these investments paid off financially.
And South Korea poured money into everything from
schools to steel plants, industrialized rapidly, and brought
down poverty.[40]

That said, the vision of development embodied in many
countries' investment programs was unrealistic or politically
distorted. Especially in the poorest nations, it was unrealistic
because it naively fixated on the most-visible aspects of
modernity—the roads and rails, dams and pipelines that
writer Catherine Caufield calls the "talismans of change." In
fact, these assets all depend on less-visible "assets" such as
skilled workers, reasonably competent government, rule of
law, an intact environment, and a fabric of small and medi-
um-sized businesses and civic organizations. These assets
were especially scarce in low-income nations, or were active-
ly undermined by the projects themselves. After
Mozambique gained independence from Portugal in the
1970s, its Ministry of Education had five people, including a

23-year-old Minister. Tanzania spent some $2 billion build-
ing roads, which disintegrated nearly as fast as they were
paved for lack of maintenance. According to a World Bank
review, 56 percent of Bank-financed projects in Africa in the
1990s ended with "satisfactory" results. But only 29 percent
were seen as likely to benefit a country's development in the
long run.[41]

Indonesia, the largest debtor among the Worldwatch 47,
has been home to some of the most financially and ecologically ruinous projects. Since the late 1980s, the country's
pulp and paper industry has expanded almost eightfold on
the strength of loans and guarantees from North American
and European ECAs wanting to stimulate exports of machinery. The industrial buildup has been financially risky, since
the companies have not arranged for an adequate, sustainable, legal supply of timber from tree plantations, according
to Christopher Barr at the Center for International Forestry
Research in Indonesia. And it has been ecologically destructive—as companies have cleared 800,000 hectares (2 million
acres) of rainforest to feed the mills, and have established
vast tree plantations on land inhabited by indigenous
peoples. The economic crisis in Indonesia has thrown the
$13 billion in overseas debt of the pulp and paper industry
into doubt. Foreign bonds of the largest company, Asia Pulp
and Paper, sold for just 40 cents on the dollar in November
2000. Yet none of the plants has shut down. Rather, some
companies are building *more* plants in order, they say, to
repay their debts.[42]

It would be unrealistic to expect countries to use every
penny of loans perfectly. Sustainable development is
extremely difficult business. And rich countries have man-
aged to develop despite their own histories of government
waste and corruption. But the losses here are large enough
that the systemic problems cannot be ignored. And they
have been occurring long enough that lenders also bear part
of the responsibility: The disappearance of funds is no secret,
nor is the inability of the poorest countries to repay their
debt. Yet it is today's debtor governments—not the lenders,

and not, in many cases, the predecessor governments that ran up the debts—that have been expected to absorb the costs by repaying loans in full.

The Devastating Spiral of Debt and Adjustment

The fact that so much of today's staggering debt was irresponsibly lent and irresponsibly borrowed would matter less if the consequences of such folly were falling on its perpetrators....Today, the heaviest burden of a decade of frenzied borrowing is falling not on the military or on those with foreign bank accounts or on those who conceived the years of waste, but on the poor who are having to do without necessities, on the unemployed who are seeing the erosion of all that they have worked for, on the women who do not have enough food to maintain their health, on the infants whose minds and bodies are not growing properly because of untreated illnesses and malnutrition, and on the children who are being denied their only opportunity ever to go to school....[I]t is hardly too brutal an oversimplification to say that the rich got the loans and the poor got the debts.

—James P. Grant, Executive Director, UNICEF, 1989[43]

The years since 1973 have been troubled ones for the global economy. Oil prices and interest rates have gyrated at times. Stock market investors and bankers have stampeded into and out of "emerging markets" from Mexico to Thailand. More subtly, rich countries have fortified their trade barriers against many principle exports of developing countries, costing them billions of dollars. In response to all these pressures, developing countries have often borrowed from foreign commercial banks, the World Bank, or the IMF, hoping this would tide them over the rough spots. But many countries, especially in Africa, instead slipped into a downward spiral:

economic hardship led to borrowing and growing debt contributed to economic crisis. Within these nations, the poor
and the environment have paid the greatest price.

The shocks and strains of the global economy during the
past quarter century have affected nations first by disrupting
their "balance of payments." When countries came to the
global market to sell their economic harvest—their copper or
coffee or cocoa—and used the proceeds to buy oil, machinery, or bank credit, their books no longer balanced. Scores of
developing countries borrowed foreign currency to get by.
Such balance-of-payments borrowing can make sense for a
government the way that living off a credit card can make
sense for a worker laid off in an industry slowdown. If the
industry recovers quickly, then the worker will get a new job
before borrowing too much; or if the cutbacks are permanent, the worker can use the line of credit to invest in training for a new career.

For the East Asian "tigers," among others, things worked
out well: they rode out the transient shocks, adjusted to the
longer-term strains, grew fast, and reduced poverty. But for
most developing countries, borrowing to balance payments
became the next stage in a dysfunctional relationship with
foreign credit. Their economies and export earnings did not
grow fast enough to keep up with the additions to their debt.
As a result, the borrowing effectively deferred tough economic choices and made those choices more painful when
they arrived.[44]

The year 1982 was a watershed in balance-of-payments
lending. Before Mexico's fateful announcement, rich-country
banks were cooperative, if increasingly nervous, providers of
ample finance to dozens of poorer nations. But afterwards,
the climate could not have been more different, as nations
from Argentina to Zambia repeatedly came within a hair of
defaulting. The world's most powerful banks, governments,
and international lending agencies presented debtors with a
solid front and a stark choice: repudiate some of their debts,
alienate great powers such as the United States, and risk losing all ability to borrow abroad for the foreseeable future—or

accept the debt burdens, and try, in the economists' word, to "adjust." Bowing to the inevitable, each troubled debtor negotiated new repayment schedules with its creditors, to cut payments in the short run. With support from the U.S. government, the IMF and the World Bank (which are international financial institutions, or IFIs) then offered the debtors new loans. But these adjustment loans were smaller than those the commercial banks had once offered, and did not relieve most governments' financial distress.[45]

In return for the new loans, the IFIs demanded that borrowers make major economic reforms, known as "adjustment," "stabilization," or "austerity" programs—in theory, the economic equivalent of retraining for the laid-off worker. In practice, the pressure to pay debts drove borrowers' economic policies as much as any blueprint drawn up by the IFIs. For like families fallen on hard times, debtor nations had few economic options. To squeeze foreign exchange out of their economies, they had to spend less or earn more. The rebalancing had to occur within each government's budget, through spending cuts or tax hikes. It also had to occur within the nation's trade flow, through higher export earnings or lower import spending.

For most adjusting countries, already reeling from balance-of-payments problems, the full-repayment-through-austerity strategy succeeded only in prolonging paralysis. Between 1950 and 1980, gross domestic product (GDP) per person had risen 105 percent in Latin America and 72 percent in Africa. But between 1980 and 1999, GDP per capita fell in Latin America and then gradually recovered for a net increase of only 4.3 percent. It fell 6.2 percent in Africa over the same period. (See Figure 5.) Statistical analysis by economist Daniel Cohen supports the conclusion that debt problems figured in the slowdown: the more vulnerable to eventual debt trouble a country seemed to be in 1980, judging by vital signs such as its ratio of foreign debt to GDP, the less it grew from then on, other factors being equal.[46]

The fundamental problem with austerity was that it put short-term goals before long-term strategies for economic

FIGURE 5

Gross Domestic Product per Person, Latin America and Africa, 1950–99

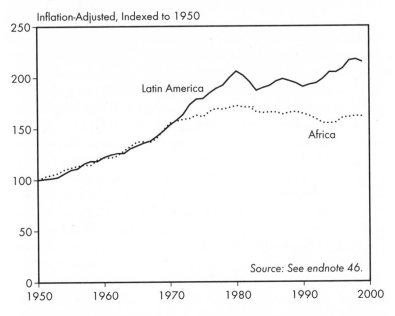

Inflation-Adjusted, Indexed to 1950

Latin America

Africa

Source: See endnote 46.

development. In countries that practiced austerity, private and public investment usually plunged. Private investors were spooked by doubts about the economic future of debtor nations. And governments preoccupied with meeting their next debt payments cut back on investment in infrastructure, health care, and education. As debtor economies ate their seed corn, output fell, unemployment climbed, and poverty spread.[47]

Another source of the growth slowdown was falling demand and sagging prices for exports of debtor nations. In the first half of 1985, for instance, Thailand exported 31 percent more rice than a year before—and earned 8 percent less. An index of the "terms of trade" of non-oil-exporting developing countries, which measures how much they could import with the earnings from a given volume of their exports, fell from 100 in 1970 to 76 in 1985, before recovering to around 85 by the late 1990s. Prices fell in part because each nation that tried to bring in more foreign exchange by increasing exports of wheat or tropical timber was competing with dozens pursuing the same strategy. In addition, rich industrial nations spent the 1980s and 1990s raising import barriers against shirts and sugar and other exports of developing countries—and subsidizing their own exports of those products. Erasing these barriers today, estimates the World Bank, would raise export earnings of developing countries by more than $100 billion a year—enough, if it had been accruing since 1982, to repay all the debts. In effect, rich countries have demanded that poor countries repay debts but refused the goods offered as payment.[48]

Like the benefits of borrowing, the costs of austerity have been spread unevenly within debtor nations. In low-income nations, where the debt crisis has arisen gradually, and is just one cause of poverty, the effects are difficult to pinpoint. In contrast, debt trouble arrived suddenly in the early 1980s in middle-income nations such as Brazil and Thailand and Turkey, which makes the link between cause and effect clearer, and hints at the effects of debt trouble elsewhere. In general, constituencies that supported the government and gained from the original loans, such as the urban middle class and ruling elites, used their influence to shift costs of repayment onto those less fortunate. There were exceptions: the poorest of the poor—such as Guatemalan Indians living in the mountains beyond paved roads and power lines—were often too isolated from the commercial economy to notice its ups and downs. And some small land-owning farmers who plugged into global markets benefited from adjustment's stimulus to exports. But they were the exceptions that proved the rule.[49]

As a group, for example, the poor appear to have suffered disproportionately from adjustment-related government cutbacks. Between 1980 and 1993, social spending fell in adjusting nations, according to a World Bank study. And within education budgets, primary education—including the one-room schoolhouses in dirt-poor hamlets—took larger cuts than universities serving urban elites. (Similar trends may have affected health budgets, but available data did not permit a clear determination.) Zaire fired a fifth of its schoolteachers in 1984, according to Susan George of the Transnational Institute. Tanzania, a country once known for nearly universal primary education, was forced to introduce school fees in 1986, thus shutting out the poorest children.[50]

Some of society's weakest members adjusted with their lives. UNICEF estimated that half a million children died each year in developing countries in the late 1980s as economic hardship slowed the long-term decline in child mortality. In northeast Brazil, where mothers struggled to feed themselves and their families, the incidence of low birth weight, which had held stable around 10.2 percent of births in the five years through 1982, jumped to 15.3 percent in 1984. Infant mortality rose too. In 1982, nine out of every 100 babies died in their first year, down from 16 in 1977. But by 1984, the figure had climbed back to 12. Meanwhile, in the southeastern state of São Paulo, government immunization cutbacks opened the way for a measles epidemic that killed thousands of babies.[51]

"Most of the burden" of adjustment... "has been borne by wage earners in the debtor countries."

In many countries, government cutbacks and recession caused layoffs and reduced the effective wages of those still working. In Mexico, inflation-adjusted wages halved between 1982 and 1988. Food prices tripled in the Jamaican capital of Kingston as subsidies were slashed. Turkey's 1980 adjustment program led to price increases for goods sold by government companies, such as gasoline and fertilizer, which effectively cut workers' wages by 45 percent between 1979 and 1985. "Most of the burden" of adjustment, concluded World Bank Chief Economist Stanley Fischer in 1989, "has been borne by wage earners in the debtor countries."[52]

The stresses of adjustment have also taken a toll on the environment, but again the story is complex. In Thailand, the government lowered tariffs to stimulate exports of rice and rubber. This encouraged farmers to shift toward those crops and away from more soil-damaging cassava farming. But it also encouraged them to clear rainforests for new rubber plantations. Economic recession slowed consumerism and cut pollution by shutting down factories in many countries. But it also drove at least a million desperately poor Filipinos into the forested mountains, where they cleared steep, erodible slopes to grow food. Likewise, poor Venezuelans splayed out along the tributaries of the Amazon to blast rocks for bits of gold.[53]

Adjustment has also taken a toll on environmental protection agencies. Nine of 12 case studies of adjusting countries commissioned by the World Wide Fund for Nature found such cuts. "In Zambia, Tanzania, and Cameroon," wrote project director David Reed, "policymakers tried to protect government employees while cutting out the funds that would allow them to perform their jobs properly....In El Salvador, environmental institutions were systematically gutted over the years." Such cuts may hurt more in the long term than the short term, since young environmental agencies in developing countries often wield little effective power, but will gain strength over time if properly supported.[54]

And the need for foreign exchange has spurred export-oriented mining, logging, and agriculture in developing countries. Several studies have found a statistical link between high debt burdens and deforestation. Debt pressure is also one reason many developing countries made their laws more inviting to foreign mining companies in the 1980s. In Tanzania, the share of mining in the country's GDP climbed 19 percent in the late 1980s.[55]

By the mid-1980s, it became clear that austerity was only prolonging and deepening most borrowers' problems with debt and adjustment. In response, the World Bank and the IMF increasingly pressed troubled debtors to make still deeper reforms in exchange for new loans—to make *structural* adjustments. If governments privatized state enterprises, ended subsidies, removed barriers to foreign trade and investment, and generally got out of the way of business, the IFIs argued, then investors would take risks again, economies would grow, and tax revenues and foreign exchange would flow into government coffers. Structural adjustment brought the anti-government economics of Reagan and Thatcher to the developing world.

Unfortunately, structural adjustment loans, like the belt-tightening austerity loans before them, mainly succeeded in perpetuating paralysis. With respect to core economic policy goals, most of the evidence says that IFI-backed adjustment programs have reduced investment, left inflation unchanged, and given at most a modest boost to economic growth and the balance of payments.[56]

In contrast with austerity programs, which had a certain inexorable logic, structural adjustment stood on shaky theoretical ground. True, countless heavy-handed government interventions were hampering economic development in many countries in the 1970s. Bloated civil services and corrupt leaders drained away revenue. Complex, constantly changing import controls bewildered traders. But it did not follow that paring government down wholesale would bring economic rebirth.

Historically, what has mattered most for development is not whether governments intervened in the workings of the economy, but the fine details of how they did so. The economies that have grown fastest in the last 200 years—including China, Japan, South Korea, and the United States—saw extensive government involvement in trade and industry. In a statistical survey of developing countries' experiences with economic growth since 1975, Harvard economist Dani Rodrik found that two factors best predicted the growth rate of an economy: how much the country invested, and whether the government held the domestic economy steady amidst the turbulence of the global economy. Keeping inflation under control and the currency's exchange rate realistic, major goals of basic austerity plans, mattered. But the openness to foreign trade and investment that *structural* adjustment aimed for—part of "globalization"—did not show up as significant by themselves.[57]

Peering deeper, the key to economic stability was political cohesion. Most governments that stabilized their economies amidst oil shocks, gyrating international interest rates, and global recession had strong mechanisms for reaching political consensus and compromise. Those mechanisms included democracy, as in South Korea and Thailand during the recent Asian economic crisis, and social programs that made almost everyone economically secure, as under the dictatorship of Singapore. Lack of social cohesion, on the other hand, led the likes of Bolivia to print money and court hyperinflation rather than confront politically risky choices about whose taxes to raise. The paths to high investment were also diverse. In some countries, private entrepreneurs took much of the initiative; in others, they were closely supervised by government planners; in still others, governments did much of the investing themselves. What mattered most was that it happened. "The lesson of history," Rodrik concludes, "is that ultimately all successful countries develop their own brand of national capitalism." When it comes to economic development, one size does not fit all.[58]

Not only was the structural adjustment advice of questionable value, it was also regularly ignored—or unnecessary. In dozens of case studies, independent economists and political scientists have documented how borrowing governments typically sidestepped the promises they made in adjustment agreements with the World Bank and the IMF, or obeyed the letter but not the spirit, or agreed to steps they would have taken anyway.[59]

The reasons for this surprising record are several. For one, as Rodrik suggests, domestic politics mainly determined economic policies. In Zambia, for example, in 1986–87, strikes by government workers and riots over a 120 percent price increase for staple foods forced the government to restore food subsidies and abandon its structural adjustment program. Bolivia, by contrast, *did* enact an adjustment program, laying off state workers and raising taxes in 1985–86—but domestic political support for drastic steps to end 50 percent-a-month hyperinflation drove these changes, not the later pressure from IFIs. Natural and human disasters also hampered compliance. In Malawi, in 1986, drought in the southern half of the country and an influx of 700,000 hungry refugees from war in Mozambique pushed the government into reversing its commitment to end fertilizer and crop subsidies. Then too, lending millions of dollars to governments uncommitted to reform bolstered forces protecting the status quo. And the IFIs' general hesitance to stop lending seriously undermined their leverage. (See "Pressure to Lend" below.)[60]

During the 1980s and 1990s, the IFIs made adjustment loans to every African nation. But according to a recent World Bank report, only two—Ghana and Uganda—sustained much commitment to reform. The authorized history of the World Bank published in 1997 concluded: "Perhaps the only argument that will convince the critics of reform [in Africa] that they are wrong will be several cases of definite structural adjustment successes...and these have not yet occurred."[61]

The main, if unintentional, effect of adjustment loans, then—for both austerity and structural adjustment—was not to transform economic policy in debt-ridden nations. Rather, it was to prolong the hope and insistence among creditors that the nations would eventually pay all their debts. This insistence left debtors staggering from one payment rescheduling agreement to the next. In the end, the pursuit of full repayment did not burnish the reputations of debtor nations among investors the way the creditors argued it would. Instead, it stymied economic growth and exacted a price measured in the misery of those least able to defend against it. And it increased the pile of unpayable debts it was meant to diminish.

Pressure to Lend

> Today marks the beginning...of a period that will be
> eventful, perhaps decisive, for us and for the world....
> [T]he United States and other like-minded nations find
> themselves directly opposed by a regime with contrary
> aims and a totally different concept of life....I believe that
> we should make available to peace-loving peoples the
> benefits of our store of technical knowledge...[a]nd
> should foster capital investment in areas needing devel-
> opment....The old imperialism—exploitation for foreign
> profit—has no place in our plans. What we envisage is a
> program of development based on the concepts of demo-
> cratic fair-dealing.
>
> —Harry S. Truman, inaugural address, 1949[62]

The first thing a good banker looks for when someone
approaches her for a loan is reassurance. That is why
"credit" derives from ancient words for "believe," "entrust,"
and "heart." Typically, a banker will ask a potential borrower for a credit history, a credible plan for using and repaying
the loan, and collateral. She will demand this reassurance
even though she, unlike a stock investor, is supposed to be
paid regardless of whether the enterprise succeeds or fails, for
she knows that borrowers sometimes fail so completely that
they go bankrupt. In the ideal, the responsible caution of the
lender counterbalances the enthusiasm of the borrower,
keeping loan losses within safe bounds and helping society
make healthy use of credit.[63]

When this balance is upset, however, credit becomes
dangerously excessive. And that is what has happened during the last several decades in the provision of finance to
poorer countries. Creditors, public and private alike, knew or
were capable of learning that much of the money they lent
was going into financially questionable uses. But creditors
too often suspended judgment, became too credulous.
Commercial lenders fell prey to the classic "go-go" psychology of financial markets. And official lenders often got

caught up in waging geopolitical battles, generating contracts for companies back home, or increasing lending for its
own sake.

Economist John Kenneth Galbraith has observed that in
commercial finance, speculative cycles share certain universal ingredients, including the "extreme brevity of the financial memory" and "the popular imagination settl[ing] on
something seemingly new in the field of commerce or
finance." Both those elements were present in the postwar
international commercial lending boom. By the late 1960s,
the retirement of bankers old enough to remember the
defaults of the 1930s enabled the historical amnesia of big
banks. And several seemingly new developments in the field
of finance appeared: the rise of the London-based
"Eurodollar" market—a regulatory twilight zone in which
banks lent to each other in a currency from one continent
while operating on another; an avalanche of "petrodollars"—deposits from conservative oil sheiks seeking the safety of big banks; and rapid economic growth in countries
such as Brazil and Kenya. The Eurodollar market became the
machinery for arranging large international loan deals.
Petrodollars provided a good share of the fuel. And developing countries that were experiencing growth spurts com-
prised the seemingly safe customer base.[64]

As the competition for market share heated up between
the likes of Chase Manhattan and the Bank of Tokyo, managers pressed their loan officers to get dollars out the door.
Author Anthony Sampson captured the mood in his descrip-
tion of the 1980 World Bank-IMF meeting, which, as a gathering of the world's finance ministers, attracted eager
bankers:

> Through the main entrance more bankers are swarming
> in, whose roving eyes suggest a very practical
> purpose....Across there a pack of Japanese bankers...is con-
> verging on a finance minister. Along the corridor a grave-
> looking French banker...looks as if he is in full pursuit of
> new African prey....Many of them begin to look not so
> much like bankers as financial middle-men, contact men,

or—could it really be?—*salesmen*....For these men who
look as if they might have been trained to say No from
their childhood are actually trying to sell *loans*. "I've got
good news for you," I heard one eager contact man telling
a group of American bankers: "I think they'll be able to
take your money."[65]

It is not hard to imagine how such lenders could have
financed, along with many good investments, much waste as
well. In 1970, commercial lenders disbursed $967 million in
long-term loans to countries that are now members of the
Worldwatch 47. By 1982, disbursements had zoomed to $10.4
billion—11 times as much. But then the crash came, and
instantly quelled the pressure to lend. Almost every year since,
commercial lenders have taken more money from these countries than they have given. Yet their outstanding commercial
debt has *risen* as interest has compounded even faster.[66]

The career of the official lenders has never been so dra-
matic. On the one hand, their slowly changing budgets and
capital quotas have generally saved them from manic
upswings in lending. On the other, their access to the richest
treasuries on earth has insulated them from losses and avert-
ed the depressive downswings.

Yet among official lenders, an array of goals have historically shouldered aside most concern about helping borrowers—and assuring their ability to repay what is lent. Most of
the tensions were audible in President Truman's inaugural
address at the dawn of the cold war. In the speech, Truman
vowed to press forward in what he cast as a biblical battle
between freedom and oppression, and called for the first-
ever peacetime foreign aid program for poor nations. Lenin,
Truman seemed to admit, had rightly condemned the West
for exploiting poor nations for their resources and enslaving
their people. To contain communism, the West had to meet
that criticism head-on, by aiding, not just exploiting, poorer
nations. With a helping hand, those nations could become
wealthier, democratic, more like the United States; and their
prosperity would ultimately benefit the West. Truman thus
voiced a mix of motives: geopolitics, missionary zeal for

democracy and capitalism, opportunities for American businesses, and a genuine desire to alleviate suffering through economic development.[67]

In practice, development frequently lost out. American determination to bankroll cold war allies and secure access to resources, for example, turned Mobutu, the Philippines' Ferdinand Marcos, and Baby Doc Duvalier into billionaires—and their governments into billion-dollar debtors. In Haiti, the U.S. government's approach was to "place maximum responsibility on the Haitian government for the selection and design of projects" even though it estimated that 63 percent of recorded revenue of the Haitian government was being "misappropriated." France's paternalism toward its former African colonies had similar results. Jean Bedel Bokassa, leader of the Central African Republic from 1966 to 1979, explained how it worked there: "Everything around here is financed by the French government. We ask the French for money, get it, and waste it."[68]

For lending governments, geopolitics often dovetailed with domestic politics. In the United States, the National Foreign Trade Council, whose members include Caterpillar, John Deere, Phillips Petroleum, and Westinghouse, lobbies for government contributions to the World Bank and other multilateral lenders, knowing they stand to gain from the resulting orders for earth-movers and power plants. But it is the bilateral export credit agencies that are the most purely political. Even people who run them say that their taxpayer-funded, industry-subsidizing loans make little overall economic sense for the lending nation—never mind the borrower. But support from companies headquartered in every major industrial nation leads to a sort of export credit arms race. "If other countries didn't do it, we wouldn't either," said the head of the Canadian ECA around 1990. "Our approach is merely to match others." Worldwide, ECAs have been major financers of arms sales. And ECAs today help keep nuclear power plant makers in business by subsidizing exports of a technology that has become uncompetitive at home.[69]

Because they are essentially bankruptcy-proof, bilateral agencies have lent for financially questionable purposes without fear. They normally lend straight from the government treasury—and pass any losses back to the treasury. In 1990, the Export-Import Bank of the United States, an ECA, admitted that a third of its loan portfolio was "delinquent"— essentially in default. This prompted the U.S. Congress to require the Ex-Im Bank to set aside $4.8 billion to cover loan losses. Suddenly, the Bank had negative net worth. "It has gone into technical insolvency," explained a former Reagan Administration official. "Not that anybody gives a damn."[70]

The financial safety nets for multilateral agencies are more complex, but are supposed to bestow equal security— and equal fearlessness. The International Bank for Reconstruction and Development (IBRD), for example, the arm of the World Bank that lends to middle-income nations, has received a cumulative $11.4 billion in capital from its shareholders, mostly governments of rich industrial countries. The IBRD has obtained an additional $176.8 billion in government guarantees—promises to deliver money should the agency ever request it. With those guarantees in hand, the IBRD has borrowed more than $100 billion from private investors at low interest rates by issuing bonds, and then lent the money on to its clients. It seems unlikely that any major member government would renege on its guarantees since financial markets would punish the government as if it had defaulted on its own bonds.[71]

This arrangement does, however, give multilateral lenders more autonomy than bilaterals have, and encourages them to lend differently. On the one hand, it partially immunizes them from outside political pressures since no one government can control them as easily as they control their own lending agencies. But the independence also leaves more room for *internal* lending pressures to grow. Truman foreshadowed this too with his expression of Saint-Simonian ideals. Making multilaterals secure and relatively independent put lending decisions in the hands of technicians hoping to do nothing less than end poverty for billions. But it also fostered a sometimes-unrealistic optimism, for real lending officials, unlike utopian ones, often did not fully understand the societies they lent to, or the risk in lending nevertheless. Training in engineering or economics fostered cookie-cutter policy prescriptions—for the same dams or structural adjustments—and frequently hindered lenders from appreciating how local culture, politics, and institutions can make a project that looks good on paper fail in practice.[72]

This is not to suggest that multilateral lenders have not, with the passage of time, come to better understand the challenges of development. They have. The problem, rather, is that they have expected borrowers to pay for this learning experience, through debt service. For its first 20 years of lending in Africa, the region where development lending has suffered the most disappointments, the World Bank targeted most of its loans at discrete projects such as highways and irrigation networks. By 1980, it saw that the approach was mostly failing: roads would be paved only to erode for lack of maintenance; schools would be erected only for poverty to force children to work more; rural development projects that aimed to improve health, education, and irrigation all at once proved too ambitious for young and corrupt borrowing agencies. The World Bank then began to focus on "institution building"—beefing up the competence of borrowing agencies—as well as structural adjustment (along with the IMF). With another 20 years of experience, Bank researchers now recognize that structural adjustment has mostly failed in Africa.[73]

Bank researchers now recognize that structural adjustment has mostly failed in Africa.

Autonomy has also given play to the bureaucratic drive for growth. No one epitomized the pursuit of growth, and the faith in its benefits, as much as Robert McNamara. Upon assuming the presidency of the World Bank in 1968, he vowed to double its lending within five years. Since then,

lending targets have sent powerful incentives down the hierarchy for speed and volume in lending, strengthening what
a high-profile World Bank report in 1992 called the loan
"approval culture." One loan officer described the culture in
the 1980s:

> When I worked on Bangladesh we decided at a country
> program division meeting that the lending program for the
> next year should be slowed, because Bangladesh could not
> absorb [use well] any more money. Everyone agreed. Then
> the division chief spoke. He said he also completely agreed.
> But if he went to his director and told him the lending
> should be slowed down, "tomorrow you will have a new
> division chief."

Bangladesh is now on Jubilee 2000's list of poor nations in
debt trouble.[74]

Growing debt troubles have compounded such pressures
to lend. Seeking to minimize the appearance of problems, the
IMF, World Bank, and regional institutions such as the
African Development Bank have often lent still more to countries struggling to service their old loans. Paul Collier, director
of the World Bank's Development Research Group, explained:
"An aid cutoff is very likely to trigger a suspension of debt service payments by the government. While the net financial
impact on the IFIs may well be the same whether they lend
money with which they are repaid or suspend lending and
are not repaid, the impact on staff careers is liable to be radi-
cally different. People do not build careers in financial institutions on default and a lack of loan disbursement."[75]

Pressure to lend still seems intense today. At the Asian
Development Bank, one anonymous and frustrated employee complained that "hierarchy is everywhere; quality control
is nowhere. This is, let's face it, a mediocre organization." At
the World Bank, the most publicly self-critical of the multilaterals, a 1997 draft internal report warned about the "pressure to lend; fear of offending the client...fear that a realistic,
and thus more modest, project would be dismissed as too
small and inadequate in its impact...and more generally, a
conviction held by many staff members that the function of

the Bank is to help create the conditions for operations to go forward, not to 'sit around and wait'." The same year, the environment-focused chapter of the authorized history of the World Bank concluded that "a majority of operational staff, in all probability, still believed there was not a strong...case for many of the Bank's [environmental] standards and procedures. Even now some still see them as...interfering in the task for which they are most rewarded: getting projects to the Board on time" for approval.[76]

This internal pressure to lend, more than any other force, explains how multilateral lenders could have financed large-scale corruption, waste, and environmental destruction. Guatemala provides one disturbing example. In the late 1970s and early 1980s, the World Bank and Inter-American Development Bank partly financed a dam on the Chixoy River. In 1980, local people whose land would be flooded by the reservoir, mostly indigenous Achi Indians, began protesting. In response, soldiers raped and tortured many villagers, then massacred 294. The World Bank "did not consider it to be appropriate to suspend disbursements." Five months after the reservoir filled, the dam stopped working because of poor design. The Bank lent another $47 million for repairs. Such problems, along with corruption, eventually raised the dam's total cost from $340 million to $1 billion and generated a substantial fraction of Guatemala's current $4.7-billion foreign debt.[77]

The story of structural adjustment lending perhaps best illustrates the weaknesses of the multilateral lenders. Not only did the IMF and the World Bank have to diagnose a country's problems, develop effective solutions, and realistically assess domestic political commitment to reform. They also needed to stop lending should the country diverge too far from the agreed path. For the most part, the IFIs have not succeeded in these tasks. (See Table 3.) As argued earlier, their economic diagnoses and prescriptions have contained valuable elements, such as the emphasis on preventing hyperinflation and keeping budget deficits in check, but have generally exaggerated the benefits of free trade and invest-

TABLE 3

Reasons IMF and World Bank Pressure for Structural Adjustment Is Weaker Than It Seems

Reason	Examples
Debt trouble	In Bolivia, debt crisis in the early 1980s led the government to print money, sparking hyperinflation and chaos. In 1985–86, a new administration adopted a harsh stabilization program that raised taxes, laid off state workers, and stopped hyperinflation. IMF and the World Bank adjustment loans came later and so contributed little to the policy shift.
Domestic politics	In Zambia, in 1986–87, strikes by government workers and riots over a 120 percent price increase for staple foods forced the government to restore food subsidies and abandon its agreed adjustment program.
Disasters	In Malawi, in 1986, drought and an influx of 700,000 refugees from civil war in Mozambique necessitated large corn imports and contributed to the government's decision to reverse commitments to end fertilizer and crop subsidies.
Finance	Adjustment lending to Argentina continued through most of the 1980s with little effect except to bolster forces for the status quo with additional funds. Withdrawal after 1988 deepened the economic crisis that soon forced reform.
Geopolitics	In the Philippines, the U.S. government, which viewed the country as an important ally, apparently pressed the IMF and World Bank to keep lending despite low compliance until the final years (1984–86) of the Ferdinand Marcos regime.
Pressure to lend and appear successful	In 1990, the World Bank promised a $100-million loan to support Kenya in ending its rationing of foreign exchange for purchasing imports. The government then resumed rationing. But local Bank officials did not alert the Bank's board for fear that it would not approve the loan. •
Multiple conditions	Among a sample of 13 sub-Saharan African nations, adjustment agreements in 1999–2000 had an average of 114 policy reform conditions each. It is unrealistic for lenders to demand complete compliance with so many conditions. Other surveys have found that countries technically comply with a typical 50–60 percent of conditions.
Ease of undermining commitments	Starting in 1984, the government of Turkey levied special taxes on imports to support extra-budgetary funds that in turn financed housing and other popular programs. This undermined but did not technically violate loan agreements to reduce conventional import tariffs and cut public investment's share of the budget.

Source: See endnote 78.

ment. And whatever the merits of structural adjustment, the IFIs' power to impose it on borrowers has been surprisingly feeble.[78]

Pressure to lend is one major factor that has weakened the IFIs' leverage. In the 1980s and early 1990s, for example, the World Bank delayed 75 percent of the second installments on its adjustment loans because borrowers were slipping on agreed reforms. (Adjustment lenders usually disburse loans in installments to extend their leverage over borrowers.) But the Bank eventually granted all but 8 percent, typically after some face-saving gesture on the part of the borrower. Similarly, the IMF abandoned half of its adjustment loans between 1979 and 1993 after the first installments—but normally then negotiated a new loan with the borrower. Sometimes the pressure to lend came from within, as Collier suggested. Other times it came from outside. A 1995 survey of 17 countries with well-documented histories of adjustment borrowing with the IMF, conducted by Tony Killick at the London-based Overseas Development Institute, found that pressure from major shareholders softened the IMF's stance in a third of the countries.[79]

IFIs have not been completely powerless to influence policy. In 1996, for example, the World Bank refused to release the second installment of an adjustment loan to Papua New Guinea because of the government's failure to make agreed anti-corruption reforms in the logging industry. The government protested bitterly, but gave in after a year, and appeared for the time being to be reforming. A World Resources Institute study credits this success to the Bank's desire to be seen fighting for the environment, to a relatively intimate understanding of local circumstances among Bank staff, and to a strong domestic constituency for reform. But such a constellation of circumstances, the authors conclude, has been rare.[80]

By the same token, it would be unfair to blame every failed loan on official or commercial lenders. Some of the projects and economic reforms they financed worked out well, especially in relatively successful countries such as

Botswana and South Korea; other loans were good bets that did not pay off.

Nevertheless, deep problems with the way lenders work have contributed to the debt crisis in low-income nations. Commercial banks' temporary bout of over-optimism made a permanent and still growing addition to countries' debt burdens. As for official lenders, many were so overtaken by external political forces that the lenders—as distinct from the people within them—effectively cared little about development and financial soundness. Even when official lenders were freer to focus on aiding borrowers, they overestimated their own ability to help. These experiences suggest that within each borrowing nation foreign lenders hoping to make a difference are best seen as one political constituency. Like every constituency, development lenders have their own peculiar goals, strategies, and tactics—and their peculiar strengths and weaknesses. Their strengths include the good intentions, training, knowledge, and ideas of their staffs, their outsider's perspective, and the money they have to offer. Their weaknesses, ironically, include those and more. For their good intentions have often made them overeager to lend. Or training in economics has diminished their appreciation of the role of culture, politics, and institutions in development. Or their outsider's perspective has blinded them to national political intrigues. Or their money has financed the forces opposed to change.

On balance, lenders are much better at pushing a country than steering it. Thus, when loans flow to countries that are developing in healthy directions, they can speed progress. But when pressure to lend puts capital in the hands of governments unlikely to use it well, Mobutu's Zaire being an extreme case, it becomes simply destructive.

Continental Drift

> [W]e must acknowledge that serious problems and impediments to a successful resolution of the debt crisis remain....Growth has not been sufficient. Nor has the level of economic policy reform been adequate. Capital flight has drained resources from debtor nations' economies.... Inflation has not been brought under control....The path towards greater creditworthiness...for many debtor countries needs to involve debt reduction.
>
> —U.S. Treasury Secretary Nicholas Brady,
> September 1988[81]

Two continents, South America and Africa, were quickly brought low by debt crisis starting in the early 1980s. But their fates then diverged. By most measures, the crisis that struck suddenly in middle-income nations during 1982 is now essentially over. In Latin America and the Caribbean, the region most severely affected, net transfers on lending (new loan receipts less payments on old loans) turned positive in 1993. A larger measure of capital flow—including investment in stock markets, factories, and office buildings—flipped from $3.4 billion outward in 1990 to $38 billion inward in 1993. Suddenly, foreign exchange was plentiful and servicing debt was much easier. Only two nations in the region—Honduras and Nicaragua—were not servicing all their foreign debts as of mid-1999, down from 17 in 1983. (See Figure 6.) But Africa, the center of the crisis in the low-income nations, remains mired in debt to this day. Nineteen African states had put servicing of some or all of their debts on hold in 1999—the same number as in 1990. Whatever it was that came to the aid of South America seemingly has yet to visit Africa.[82]

Africa and Latin America began to drift apart in the late 1980s. What sent them on different trajectories? In a word, compromise. Commercial creditors, which dominate lending to Latin America, were much quicker to compromise than were official creditors, which dominate lending to

FIGURE 6

Number of Countries Not Servicing All Their Foreign Debts, by Region, 1970–99

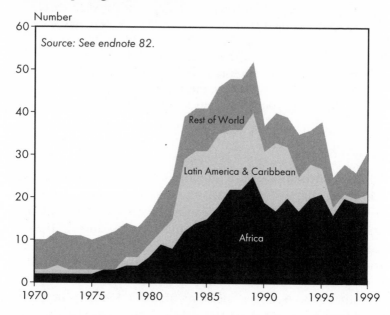

Africa. In March 1988, for example, Bolivia's commercial creditors agreed to sell half the country's IOUs back to Bolivia for 6 cents on the dollar. Commercial creditors, in other words, accepted a 94 percent loss in exchange for wiping bad loans to one small nation off their books. And some creditors swapped their old bank loans for new bonds with easier repayment terms. For instance, Argentina arranged with banks to replace some of its debts with bonds that had the same face value, but an interest rate of just 4 percent and a 25-year repayment schedule, including a 12-year grace period. In another type of deal, a debt-for-equity swap, Argentina retired $5 billion in debt in 1990 by giving banks its national airline and its phone company.[83]

Nonprofit organizations began arranging deals of their own, on a smaller scale. One kind, debt-for-nature swaps, worked like this: In August 1987, the U.S. group Conservation International (CI) bought Bolivian debt with a face value of $650,000 from commercial banks. Because the banks viewed the loans as nearly worthless, they sold the debt for only $100,000. CI cancelled $400,000 of the debt and accepted the remaining $250,000 in Bolivian currency rather than dollars, which were scarce in Bolivia. The group then donated the proceeds for management of Bolivia's 15,000-square-kilometer Beni Biosphere Reserve. In effect, Bolivia paid off loans by "exporting" the service of protecting its forests to the rest of the world, rather than exporting the trees.[84]

Soon other environmental groups joined in, making deals with Honduras, Madagascar, Zambia, and two dozen other nations. Over time, bilateral aid agencies became the major players—though not on a scale that could end any debt crisis. To date, donors have retired some $7 billion in debt and freed up more than $1 billion for environmental projects. (Half of the write-offs have gone to Poland, where an "EcoFund" is cleaning up some of the worst environmental legacies of the communist era.) In the same vein, UNICEF bought or received donations of debt with a face value of $200 million between 1989 and 1995, which it used to finance debt-for-development swaps. The goals of projects funded ranged from providing clean water in Sudan to helping street children in Jamaica.[85]

The growing acceptance of such deals among banks allowed the U.S. government to change its position on the debt crisis. In 1988, Treasury Secretary Nicholas Brady publicly described the outgoing Reagan administration's insistence on full repayment through adjustment as a failure. The key to resolution, he said, was compromise—just as it had been in every debt crisis before. Under the Brady Plan, announced in early 1989, each debtor nation gave its commercial lenders a menu of choices. One option was to lend more money to cover payments coming due. Another was for the bank to tear up some of its IOUs in exchange for new ones. The new IOUs could have the same principal as the old ones but a lower interest rate, like those Argentinean bonds.

Or the promised interest payments could stay low for a few years and then climb. Payments could even be tied to the price of the country's exports: when export earnings rose, banks would share in the gains, like stockholders.[86]

One option that was not on the banks' menus was to *not* compromise. If it had been, then Citibank, for example, might have waited for Deutsche Bank to strike a deal with Brazil, accept a loss, and help Brazil regain creditworthiness—at which point Citibank would have demanded full repayment. But Deutsche Bank and other competitors, of course, would have waited too. In the ban on doing nothing lay the genius of the Brady Plan.[87]

Between 1990 and 1994, debtors including Argentina, Brazil, Mexico, Nigeria, and the Philippines struck Brady agreements, in each case ending years of repeated, crisis-atmosphere negotiations. The compromises gave borrowing governments financial breathing room, lifted the atmosphere of uncertainty, brought investment back, and helped rekindle economic growth. As a result, middle-income nations have serviced their debts more easily since the early 1990s.[88]

Creditor governments, however, showed less interest in compromise than private bankers. In Venice, in June 1987, leaders of the G–7 nations made their first accommodation to the debt troubles in the poorest nations. They agreed to let debtors defer payments on outstanding loans, provided they stuck to structural adjustment agreements with the IMF. At succeeding summits, the G–7 gradually offered more, but to no avail. The failure of their newer offers could be measured throughout the 1990s by the stagnating or worsening indebtedness indicators of the poorest nations.[89]

Creditor governments delayed confronting the official debt crisis mainly because they could get away with it. They maximized their bargaining power by presenting a solid front, through an informal institution called the Paris Club, while insisting on negotiating with debtors one at a time. "[T]he Paris Club has generally been able to rally its members in a relatively short time along the lines of interpreting reschedulings as extraordinary short-term measures that should not be confused with development efforts," explains sociologist Christian Suter. Especially after the cold war ended, most debtors were in no position to push for concessions.[90]

As a result, political battles within rich nations have generally determined how their governments have responded to the debt problems of poor nations. Just recently, the political balance has shifted decisively in favor of quick cancellation. In 1996, British Christian aid groups launched one of the most successfully organized international movements ever: the Jubilee 2000 campaign. By 2000, more than 100 organizations belonged, ranging from small nongovernmental groups in Uganda to dozens of local, church-based chapters to heavyweights such as Oxfam. They demanded that creditors cancel debt immediately and that debtors use the savings to fight poverty. The campaign gained clout from the 24 million signatures on its petitions, and endorsements from Pope John Paul II, the Dalai Lama, and U2 lead singer Bono. And it drew strength from the Bible's Book of Leviticus, which records God's laws for ancient Israel. Leviticus declared that every 50th year was to be a year of Jubilee, in which creditors forgave debtors and farmers reclaimed land they had sold off to survive a bad year. Such redistribution was intended to prevent extreme inequalities from arising to tear the fabric of Israelite society.[91]

Jubilee 2000 scored a major victory at the G–7 summit in 1999 when official creditors announced the enhanced HIPC initiative. The initiative, which is administered by the IMF and the World Bank, represents an artful political compromise among the opponents and proponents of quick cancellation, and multilateral lending agencies as well. The initiative bows to Jubilee's demand by promising that bilateral and multilateral creditors alike will write off substantially more debt than before—up to 45 percent, on average, for 41 qualifying nations. It also requires each debtor to first design a Poverty Reduction Strategy Paper (PRSP) in consultation with civil society groups, such as NGOs and churches, and then to implement the strategy with savings from debt cancellation. But by requiring structural adjustment, the

HIPC initiative accommodates those skeptical about writing blank checks to dictators. And it helps the multilaterals by partially reimbursing them (through a HIPC Trust Fund) for canceling debt. Finally, it attempts to head off criticism of official lenders by casting the write-offs more as a one-time act of generosity than an unavoidable consequence of ongoing problems.[92]

In addition, Canada, Italy, the United Kingdom, the United States, and other countries have individually offered to write off all their loans to poor debtors, which could bring the total reduction to 55 percent. Most of these offers piggyback on the HIPC initiative: to take advantage of them, countries must first qualify for the initiative.[93]

But offers that work politically may not work in practice. The question remains: Will these initiatives do for Africa (and other low-income debtors) what the Brady Plan did for South America? Or will the two continents continue to drift apart?

The Year of Jubilee?

> When national debts have once been accumulated to a certain degree, there is scarce, I believe, a single instance of their having been fairly and completely paid.
>
> —Adam Smith, *The Wealth of Nations,* 1776[94]

It has been 225 years since Adam Smith remarked that he had hardly heard of a heavily indebted government repaying in full. Almost 175 years have passed since the first modern wave of defaults rolled across Latin America. Half a century has elapsed since President Truman launched the modern official lending enterprise with great hope for development and freedom. It was just under two decades ago that Mexico's finance minister walked into the U.S. Treasury and turned his pockets inside out, just over a decade since Secretary Brady embraced compromise. And it is a mere moment in the sweep of history since the year 2000, the Year of Jubilee, came to a close, leaving the present with a persisting debt crisis in the world's poorest places, and some impressive promises to end it. The history of sovereign debt trouble is long: it has much to teach. And today's debt problems are urgent: there is great need to learn from the past.

The current debt crisis poses two problems: how to treat the symptoms, and how to cure the illness. Because recent debt reduction initiatives are one-time offers, they only treat the symptoms. They are the focus of this section. The search for a cure is the focus of the next.

History teaches three key lessons on how to end a debt crisis once it arises:

First, compromise is necessary. Resolution through compromise has been the norm throughout modern international debt history. Each of the major crises in the 1820s, 1870s, and 1930s led to deals for partial repayment. Angry creditors had to accept that no matter how unfair it might be, the most they could get back was a fraction of their money and a valuable lesson. Similarly, when a new government came to power on the borrowing side, it almost always had to make some payments on debts contracted by its predecessor if it was to regain the confidence of foreign lenders. Under the Brady Plan, too, realistic compromise served *both* sides far more than stern demands for full repayment had.

Second, humility is important. Development projects, including adjustment programs, fail as much as they succeed, and sometimes they do outright harm. Processes of economic development are extremely complex and the barriers to progress many. Demanding too much change too fast can backfire.

Third, speed is vital. Continuing crisis imposes a cost on debtors, in lost jobs and lower wages, in cleared forests and children's lives.

In light of these principles, the recent debt cancellation offers are steps in the right direction, representing a major shift in approach to the official debt crisis by apparently recognizing the value of compromise, humility, and speed. But they still fall short in their particulars. The political bargain they embody offers something to each constituency that shaped it, but works less well as policy.

Recent debt reduction offers make a deep bow in the direction of compromise. By the end of 2000, some 22 nations had entered the HIPC initiative, and won promises to cut their debts from $53 billion to $20 billion—a substantial 62 percent cut. Fifty-five percent of this comes from the HIPC initiative, and 7 percent from offers piggybacked on it. But the creditors concede less than appearances suggest. For example, the HIPC initiative does not compromise with Indonesia, Nigeria, and Pakistan. It excludes them even though they are as indebted and poor as eligible nations. Why? They are judged by the World Bank to be too creditworthy. Yet each is either unrated by Moody's and Standard and Poor's, which means that commercial creditors mostly avoid the country, or it is rated *less* creditworthy than eligible countries that *are* rated. Pakistan, for example, receives a B– from S&P, while HIPC-eligible Bolivia and Senegal each get a B+. It is perhaps not a coincidence that Indonesia, Nigeria, and Pakistan are the largest debtors among the Worldwatch 47. To grant them comparable debt relief, creditors would need to take tens of billions of dollars more in losses onto their books. (Among the Worldwatch 47, Afghanistan is also excluded because it has cut off most contact with foreign creditors; and Cambodia and Comoros are omitted because they can get comparable debt relief from programs established before the HIPC initiative.)[95]

In addition, the HIPC initiative's definition of "sustainable debt"—the amount of debt a country is supposed to be able to manage—still appears to be high. Indeed, World Bank and IMF staff have admitted the criteria are rather arbitrary. For example, the HIPC initiative aims to cap a country's annual debt service payments at 15–20 percent of export earnings. By comparison, the victors in World War I demanded that Germany pay 13–15 percent of its exports in reparations, and that was enough to stoke nationalist anger and help Hitler to power. After World War II, West Germany's creditors learned from history and settled for 3.5 percent of exports, so as not to slow the nation's recovery. The world's poorest nations deserve at least as much consideration.[96]

Even with the 41 eligible countries, recent offers compromise less than appearances suggest. If the countries can only repay 31 percent of their debts, as economist Daniel Cohen implies, and are only maintaining the appearance of servicing the debts by borrowing still more in a sort of money merry-go-round, then demanding 45 percent repayment will not make much difference. After creditors take this big step toward realism, debtors will be pressed almost as hard as before to service their debts, and will spend almost as much over the long run doing so. The main effect will be to slash the amount of money going around in circles.[97]

Recent projections from the World Bank tend to corroborate Cohen's predictions. Though the HIPC program should cut the debts of the 22 countries that have so far entered it by 55 percent, it will reduce their annual debt service payments by only 31 percent, from $3.0 billion a year in 1998–99 to $2.1 billion in 2001–05. Even this figure probably overstates the immediate benefits: if new lending to these countries goes down as the money merry-go-round slows, then the countries will receive even less on net.[98]

The HIPC initiative also shows a sort of humility. This it does by requiring debtor governments to work with nongovernmental groups on plans to fight poverty with savings from debt relief. Through this condition, lenders are tacitly admitting that they and borrowing governments do not hold a monopoly on wisdom and information about fighting poverty. Uganda began such a consultation in 1995 and offers an example of the benefits: it shifted funding toward providing safe drinking water in response to comments from poor communities. When creditors endorse such a consultation, it gives civil society organizations "the legitimacy to stand up and say, 'is this policy action going to reduce poverty in my country?'" observes the Brussels-based European Network on Debt and Development (EURODAD). By supporting such voices, the Poverty Reduction Strategy Paper requirement could make a subtle but valuable contribution to the political and economic development of borrowing nations over the long term.[99]

But again, important details undermine the appearance of change. First, the new requirement joins rather than replaces old ones: debtors are also supposed to stick to a standard structural adjustment plan for three to six years to obtain permanent debt reduction. Indeed, according to NGOs polled by EURODAD, most local IMF representatives still seem to care more about structural adjustment than poverty reduction strategies. Debtor governments are taking the cue, emphasizing measures such as privatization of state companies in their economic plans.[100]

Second, PRSP requirements are hardly humble. They fail to take into account the complex relationship between paper promises and actual policy changes. A consultation process raises questions akin to those confronted by drafters of a constitution, points out Joan Nelson, a political scientist at American University in Washington, D.C. Who should participate? Churches? NGOs based in the capital? Elected leaders of certain villages? What is a legitimate process for selecting participants? Once selected, should participants have a veto, a vote, or just a voice? For officials on the debtor side, who must design the processes, these questions are among the most politically charged they could ask. For officials on the creditor side, who must judge the process, the questions are hard to answer with confidence. A report by the U.S. General Accounting Office (GAO) gives a sense of the tensions:

> [I]n 1997 the government of Bolivia conducted a "national dialogue" to involve civil society in its effort to build support for its new economic and social priorities. Although government officials considered that effort to have been quite worthwhile, some nongovernmental organizations and donors...disagreed. They told us the dialogue consisted of a 1-day meeting in which the government selected whom to invite, involved little regional participation, little background information, and used the meeting

to present its views. One nongovernmental organization representative characterized this effort as having been more a "regional monologue than a national dialogue."

(The HIPC initiative has spurred the government of Bolivia to organize a second, more inclusive consultation, one that may prove more worthy of the PRSP label.)[101]

It would be hard to design debt cancellation conditions more likely to engender domestic political opposition and more difficult to enforce. Debtors uncommitted to poverty reduction—or less responsive to pressure from civil society—may put on disingenuous PRSP shows in order to obtain debt relief, as NGOs in Kenya fear is happening there. On the other hand, debtors that are committed to helping the poor will probably owe their commitment much more to their own history and leadership than to outside pressure. Certainly this is the case in Ghana and Uganda.[102]

Finally, the PRSP requirements seem naive to the complexities of poverty itself. It takes time, especially for a cash-strapped government, to assess the extent and nature of poverty, consult with the groups affected—from slum dwellers to landless farmers—then assign priorities to potential responses and draw up plans. Ghana and Uganda had been working on their schemes for five years as of mid-2000.[103]

Herein lies a central tension in the HIPC initiative. History teaches that speed is vital in resolving debt crises. But developing good plans takes time. The PRSP requirements could delay debt reduction for years while countries assemble high-quality plans. Or governments could ram strategies through superficial consultations in order to win quick debt relief.

Recognizing the problem, the initiative's designers allow debtors to submit interim poverty plans in return for prompt but provisional debt relief in the form of lower annual debt payments. Permanent reductions in the debt stock are to come several years later, upon approval of a full PRSP. But this approach does not eliminate the tension over tempo. In 2000, for example, the government of Honduras decided to shoehorn initial consultations with civil society into a few months so that it could submit an interim PRSP by March 2001. But once interim poverty reduction plans receive the stamp of approval of the IMF and the World Bank, they can take on a life of their own. Burkina Faso's final PRSP closely follows the interim one, for example, which was drafted after little public consultation.[104]

The thinking among official lenders about how to respond to the debt crisis took a major step forward with the enhanced HIPC initiative. But from the standpoint of realism, recent debt reduction offers still give too little and ask too much. The irony is that the official debt crisis is, in a sense, easy to solve. Of the $422 billion in debt of the Worldwatch 47, all but perhaps $130 billion has, for purposes of repayment, probably disappeared forever. Financially, all that is at stake now is how much of the $130 billion creditors should forgive. Canceling half would cost $65 billion, once. That is not a lot of money in the scheme of things. Every 100 days, the U.S. government pays $65 billion in interest on its own debt. Every 50, Western governments spend that much on weapons and armies. Thus, if NGOs and religious leaders continue campaigning for cancellation and creditors continue to respond, it is only a matter of time before much of the debt burden is lifted from the poorest countries.[105]

The greater challenge is to prevent a new burden from growing in its place.

What To Do about Lending

The policy of reducing Germany to servitude for a generation, of degrading the lives of millions of human beings, and of depriving a whole nation of happiness should be abhorrent and detestable...even if it did not sow the decay of the whole civilized life of Europe. Some preach it in the name of justice. In the great events of man's history, in the unwinding of the complex fates of nations Justice is not so simple. And if it were, nations are not authorized, by religion or by natural morals, to visit on the children of their enemies the misdoings of parents or of rulers.

—John Maynard Keynes, *The Economic Consequences of the Peace*, 1919[106]

The Versailles peace conference of 1919 brought the "war to end all wars" to an official close. The victors redrew the map of Europe and imposed billions of dollars in demands for war reparations on the principle loser, Germany. After witnessing the negotiations firsthand, the British economist John Maynard Keynes stormed home and penned those prescient lines. Much as he feared it would, the heavy debt soon destabilized Germany's new democratic government. It contributed to the decision to print money to pay bills, to hyperinflation, to the rise of Hitler, and to the splintering of the industrial world into rival alliances. Within a generation, the war to end all wars had to be renamed World War I. And Germany's problem with debt had become the world's.[107]

The debt burden behind the current crisis almost certainly will not lead to world war. But there is no question that, like the demands placed on Germany in 1919, it is immoral and impossible. By entangling creditors and borrowers in endless contention, squeezing public investment in infrastructure and people, and scaring off private investors, it is impeding economic development, aggravating poverty, and doing irreparable damage to the environment. And when so many countries struggle, it can only harm the rest of the world. The situation demands an effective and rapid response.

The first order of business is to build on recent debt reduction offers and end the current crisis. If creditors take to heart the lessons from history on the value of compromise, humility, and speed, they will swiftly and unconditionally cancel all debt that seems unpayable—which is most of it. Critics will call such sweeping cancellations "blank checks." But in effect the lenders have already written those blank checks by making loans that cannot be repaid. Here, the governments of Canada, the United Kingdom, and the United States are leading the way by regularly evaluating the creditworthiness of their borrowers and estimating how much they will repay on outstanding debts. The United States, for example, had written off 91 percent of its loans to the HIPC 41 by mid-2000.[108]

The question of how creditors should handle the remaining, *payable* debt is connected to the larger question of how best to aid development. Experience strongly suggests that canceling payable debt of the most despotic governments—like granting them new loans—will do little good. In some cases, cancellation will only bolster the dominant political forces arrayed against reform. On the other hand, canceling payable debt of governments that seem committed to reform could allow them to effectively invest millions more dollars each year in needed roads or schools or water supplies. Requiring debtors to go through a PRSP-like process could make a modest difference by bolstering domestic coalitions for reform. But overall, the choice of whose payable debt to cancel will matter more than what conditions are imposed in exchange.

There can be no simple formulas for predicting which countries will put savings from cancellation of payable debt to good use. Instead, people who know a debtor nation well will have to exercise their judgment in light of the country's current political and economic climate, the state of its institutions, and its history. Most observers agree that Uganda, for instance, stands a good chance of making the most of debt cancellation, by managing its economy and investing in poverty reduction with competence. Creditors should make sure that they do not create institutional pressures to cancel payable debt that, like pressures to lend, would override the judgment of professionals in the field.

There is little cause for worry that writing off so much debt would bankrupt multilateral lenders or harm their credit ratings. Except for the African Development Bank, all major multilateral lenders have enough reserves to write off *all* of their IOUs from the HIPC 41, for example. Lenders can also call in guarantees, the contributions that shareholder governments have already promised to deliver on demand. (See Figure 7.)[109]

Such a realistic and straightforward approach would quickly end the debt crisis—but only for a while. For if lending continues as before, billions more dollars will disappear in the familiar ways, and debt burdens will once again rise faster than ability to repay. Relief may rewind countries a few

FIGURE 7

Multilateral Lenders: Total Assets and Cumulative Loans to 41 Heavily Indebted Poor Countries, End of 1998

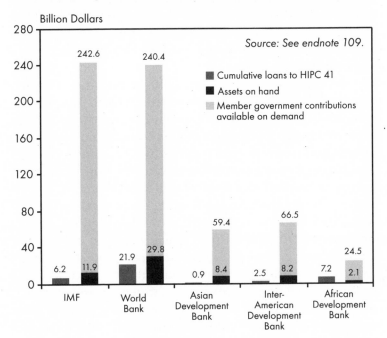

Billion Dollars

Source: See endnote 109.

■ Cumulative loans to HIPC 41
■ Assets on hand
▨ Member government contributions available on demand

decades debt-wise, but without deeper changes, the same borrowing tape will play again. The GAO has crafted a mathematical model of Tanzania, for example, which suggests that after the HIPC initiative cuts the country's foreign debt from $5.7 billion to about $1.8 billion the country will then borrow enough to lift its debt back to $6.4–7.3 billion by 2018. For if Tanzania shifts spending from debt service to social services—as it is supposed to under the HIPC initiative—it will need as much revenue as before. Unless tax revenues or foreign grants rise, Tanzania will need to borrow just as much each year as it used to. And the new debt will be unpayable unless the economy and exports grow improbably fast.[110]

This projection points to the greatest shortcoming in recent attempts to end the debt crisis: they do far too little to change the systems that created the crisis in the first place. Indeed, by casting write-offs as one-time acts of generosity, they bury uncomfortable questions about how creditors could have made so many bad loans. Bringing a lasting end to the debt crisis and shaping a healthy relationship between debt and development will take more than political leaders pledging to wipe away the worst signs of past failures. It will take fundamental reforms in the way rich countries relate financially to poor ones.

Four key problems lie at the heart of the crisis. The first is that rich industrial countries restrict imports from developing countries, yet poor debtors have to repay their foreign loans in foreign currency, which they can only earn by exporting. Governments in rich industrial countries channel $326 billion a year in subsidies toward their own farmers— enough to pay off the debt of the Worldwatch 47 in 16 months. During the Uruguay Round negotiations that resulted in a new General Agreement on Tariffs and Trade (GATT) and founded the World Trade Organization in 1994, these subsidies were one of the toughest sticking points between industrial countries and poorer ones that could not afford the same protection for their own farmers. In the end, rich countries promised to cut subsidies only 20 percent from high late-1980s levels. Protectionism for textile makers emerged relatively intact too. It seems that only the rich members of the global community are allowed to knock down foreign barriers to their exports. In 2000, Michel Camdessus, head of the IMF, declared that "this failure, unless quickly reversed, would make a mockery of a decision on debt [the HIPC initiative] that is, otherwise, of historic dimensions."[111]

There are some hopeful signs of change. In May 2000, President Clinton signed the Africa Growth and Opportunity Act into law. Under the slogan "trade not aid," the new law pried open the United States' Byzantine regulations of textile imports. As of January 2001, fully 35 African nations were eligible to export fabric and clothing to the United States with fewer restrictions and tariffs than in the past. The U.S. government estimates that imports from these countries could rise from $250 million to $4 billion by 2008. However, it remains to be seen how much of those earnings will flow to government coffers, or to African workers, as opposed to textile factory owners. And the act hardly marks an end to discriminatory protectionism against the poorest countries. Nevertheless, the move does suggest that rich nations are becoming more willing to compromise on trade barriers for the sake of economic development overseas.[112]

The second problem behind the debt crisis is that agencies that lend and borrow have seldom let worries about ability to repay stop them from arranging a loan. Fortunately, one major source of pressure to lend—the cold war—has evaporated. But another is as strong as ever: the mutually supportive relationship between major exporting companies and contractors on the one hand and official lenders, especially export credit agencies, on the other. The best hope for ending the ECA arms race lies in international negotiations on the lending equivalent of an arms reduction treaty, perhaps an addition to GATT, which would require all signatories to simultaneously scale back their export financing. To date, GATT negotiators have specifically exempted ECAs from most rules limiting government control of trade, no doubt reflecting the political clout of exporting companies.

But such pressures always oppose trade liberalization and, in spite of them, industrial countries have reduced many tariffs substantially in the postwar era. Here, too, there is hope for eventual progress.[113]

The third problem is a fundamental mismatch between lending and development. Loans are expected to be repaid. But development projects can be expected to fail regularly. Aiding sustainable development in another country is extremely difficult. Aid agencies can point to some major successes, including the eradication of smallpox and a rapid drop in family size in developing countries brought about in substantial part by donor-funded family planning programs. But overall, it is indigenously driven reforms, such as the shifts toward the market in China and government-led investment in South Korea, that have generated most of the successes in the global war on poverty.[114]

This mismatch raises a provocative question: Why lend? Why should aid agencies lend their money to the poorest countries rather than grant it? One argument for lending is that it instills a sense of responsibility in borrowing governments—the same lesson a father hopes to teach when he lends, rather than gives, his teenage son the money to buy a stereo. Decades of experience, however, show that the paternalism metaphor is inapt. Successful political leaders in borrowing countries, like successful leaders everywhere, are generally pragmatic to the detriment of their countries. Their time horizons are often more short term than the maturities of the loans they accept. Thus, domestic politics largely determines how well they use foreign money, whether lent or granted.

Another argument for lending is that a rich government that is willing to grant a poor one only $10 million, say, might stand ready to lend $100 million, which could mean more vaccines or schools for the borrower. But loans are not a free lunch: they boost a borrower's budget in the short run and squeeze it in the long run. A final, related argument is that loan repayments from countries that are successfully developing can be recycled to poorer ones. But among the poorest debtors at least, the arrangement is backfiring. So bad has the problem become that in 2000 Malawi turned down a loan offer from the World Bank for fighting AIDS, on the grounds that the loan would add to the debt burden that is itself hobbling government efforts to combat the disease.[115]

Reasoning along these lines has led most bilateral aid agencies, with the prominent exception of Japan, to stop lending. To be consistent, governments should convert multilateral lending programs that target the poorest countries to grant-making as well.[116]

Since the conversion probably will not happen immediately, the question remains of how to make development lending work better. Recognizing their limited influence over borrowing countries, development lenders will reduce the mismatch if they favor countries that seem most committed to reform and progress. The World Bank has taken this principle to heart in its new Higher Impact Adjustment Lending program, which concentrated $2 billion in lending during 1996–98 on 17 African nations, in a sort of triage process. Recipient nations performed better during this time than other African countries in terms of inflation, economic growth, and ability to keep up with their foreign debt. Whether the lending led to this better performance, or the other way around, the Bank's studies suggest that the funds were probably put to better overall use than if they had been spread evenly across the continent.[117]

Indigenously driven reforms have generated most of the successes in the global war on poverty.

More fundamentally, managers at lending agencies need to rein in the pressure to lend, to reward employees more for results and less for loan output. Unfortunately, it is hard to assess the ultimate benefits of an aid project. If an aid agency finances construction of an elementary school and poverty falls a generation later, does the agency deserve credit? Moreover, in retrospect even risks that do not pay off may have been worth taking at the time. But judging quality is not impossible: at the World Bank, the Operations Evaluation Department has been doing it since the early 1970s. Nor should it be impossible to improve on present management, which puts such overbearing stress on output. The realistic goal is improvement, not perfection.[118]

Even this goal may be ambitious since official lenders do not have a strong record of reforming themselves. World Bank management, for example, has recognized the problem of pressure to lend for a decade, but has not reduced it. It is hard to escape the conclusion that lenders will not tackle the problem until circumstances force them to. Their insularity from the costs of their own decisions is precisely what has allowed the pressure to flourish.

This insularity, this lack of accountability, constitutes the fourth major cause of the debt crisis in the poorest nations. The problem is as easy to state as it is difficult to correct. The history of structural adjustment lending shows just how hard it can be for outsiders to force an institution to change—and to ensure that whatever pressure they apply does more good than harm. If member governments were to take the extreme step of privatizing multilateral lenders, for example, so that the lenders became fully responsible for their own bottom lines, then the lenders might get caught up in the same fads as commercial banks, pouring money into the continent of the decade, then yanking it out even faster—precisely the behavior that has generated commercial debt crises for two centuries.

More judicious measures, however, could give lenders a dose of pressure and criticism that, however unpleasant, would be ultimately healthy. One intriguing option would be to partly tie loan repayments to the increase in the borrower's GDP or exports. Lenders would then become more like stock market investors, standing to lose in the event of failure—or to reap high returns in the event of success. Strange as it may seem to link loan payments to GDP or exports, the HIPC initiative already does exactly that by capping a country's public-debt-to-exports ratio at 150 percent. And some bonds issued under the Brady Plan work the same way. Applying the practice to new loans would just make it less ad hoc.

In addition, creditor governments can scale back or eliminate the HIPC Trust Fund. Financed by creditor governments, the trust fund is partially reimbursing development banks for writing down debt under the HIPC initiative. But when governments of developing countries bail out insolvent private banks, economists working for lending agencies worry about the "moral hazard" this creates by effectively rewarding and encouraging bad lending decisions. Similarly, the trust fund partially insulates multilateral lenders from past mistakes and thus entrenches the management that led to those mistakes. Moreover, as pointed out above, the trust fund is unnecessary. Lenders already have all the capital they require to cover any losses. On balance, the trust fund creates a strange asymmetry in the HIPC initiative: debtors must jump through hoops for their small amount of true debt relief while multilateral lenders get their money unconditionally. In this sense, the initiative is designed by and for creditors.

Looking ahead, governments can base their new contributions to each multilateral lender in part on how effectively each one appears to be grasping the nettle of internal reform. Just as with government borrowers, giving preferential treatment to lenders that *are* reforming, rather than those that have merely promised to reform, will likely work best in the long run. Scaling back the HIPC Trust Fund or slowing new contributions to some multilaterals would mean less lending to poor countries in the short run. But given the lenders' problematic record, of which the official debt crisis is one symptom, it is more important now to improve the steering of lending, by prodding the multilateral banks to reform, than to press the accelerator pedal.

Finally, governments need to create an international government bankruptcy process. Ad hoc responses such as the HIPC initiative are most useful if they evolve into more systematic, permanent approaches. National bankruptcy codes, for example, embody centuries of experimentation and refinement of just this sort.

A sovereign bankruptcy system, established under international treaty, could systematically and speedily allocate losses among the parties. All countries would be eligible to seek its protection. Once the process was invoked, creditors and debtors could each appoint, say, two judges to a bankruptcy panel, who would in turn choose a fifth, suggests Austrian economist Kunibert Raffer. The panel could estimate how much debt would never be repaid and cancel it, without imposing conditions for structural adjustment or poverty reduction. Just as in a commercial bankruptcy, this would be an act of realism, not charity. If the debtor government had recently moved from dictatorship toward democracy, the panels might also cancel "odious" debts, on the grounds that debts contracted to harm the people should not be paid by the people. In the future, official lenders might lend more cautiously, knowing that borrowing nations could seek bankruptcy protection.[119]

Given the political and practical complexities of lending and development, no one of these proposals nor any combination will completely solve the problems at hand. The most effective reform strategy will therefore blend many approaches to forestall, if not completely prevent, the next crisis.

History offers one last lesson: reforms do not enact themselves. Most credit for recent progress on the debt crisis goes to nongovernmental organizations. It is they who aroused and channeled pressure from religious leaders, pop stars, and millions of activists and citizens around the world. It is they who pushed creditor governments along the road to realism. It is they who spotlighted the Year of Jubilee. Yet their impressive, if partial, success is child's play next to the job of preventing fresh debt troubles. Most of the needed changes—tearing down certain trade barriers, reining in ECAs, and curtailing development lending to the poorest nations—are tasks for which the blunt power of righteous activists is suited. Reforming development lenders, however, will take more than bare-fisted political battles—though it will take that. Somehow, NGOs also need to work with lending agencies toward goals they share, so that managers and rank and file at the agencies come to feel committed to the reforms, rather than just besieged.

The jubilee has not arrived yet. But if all those committed to bringing it about work hard and well, it will. And like the jubilees promised in the Bible, this emancipation will be spectacular enough to banish debt troubles for generations to come.

Notes

Many sources cited here are available on the Internet even when not so indicated.

1.   Randall Arlin Fegley, "Congo, Democratic Republic of the," in *Microsoft Encarta Encyclopedia 2000* (Redmond, WA: Microsoft Corporation, 1999).

2.   Ibid.; Anthony Sampson, *The Money Lenders: Bankers in a World of Turmoil* (New York: Viking Press, 1982), pp. 150–54; Susan George, *A Fate Worse Than Debt: The World Financial Crisis and the Poor* (New York: Grove Press, 1988), p. 114; U.S. aid from Rosie DiManno, "Unleash the Dogs of War...and They Devour a City," *Toronto Star*, 5 July 2000; Jimmy Burns, Mark Huband, and Michael Holman, "Mobutu Built a Fortune of $4bn from Looted Aid," *Financial Times*, 12 May 1997.

3.   Crash from Sampson, op. cit. note 2, p. 151; repeated reschedulings from Christian Suter, *Debt Cycles in the World-Economy: Foreign Loans, Financial Crises, and Debt Settlements, 1820–1990* (Boulder, CO: Westview Press, 1992), p. 71, and from World Bank, *Global Development Finance 2000*, vol. 1 (Washington, DC: 2000), pp. 162, 181; default from idem, *Annual Report 2000*, Financial Statements and Appendixes to the Annual Report (Washington, DC: 2000), p. 88, and from International Monetary Fund (IMF), *Annual Report 2000* (Washington, DC: 2000), p. 190; hunger from George, op. cit. note 2, pp. 106–08.

4.   Total debt from World Bank, *Global Development Finance 2001*, advance release (electronic database) (Washington, DC: 2001); population from U.S. Bureau of the Census, International Data Base, electronic database, Suitland, MD, 10 May 2000; income from World Bank, *World Development Indicators* (electronic database) (Washington, DC: 2000).

5.   Figure of $855—the current "operational cutoff" for access to the World Bank's International Development Association (IDA) loans—and GNP per capita figures from World Bank, *Annual Report*, op. cit. note 3, pp. 128–29. Exports and present value of public and publically guaranteed debt are Worldwatch estimates, based on idem, *Global Development Finance*, op. cit. note 3, pp. 144–46, and on idem, *Global Development Finance*, op. cit. note 4. Count of 47 includes: Bolivia, whose GNP per capita is above $855, but which is not considered creditworthy enough to borrow from the World Bank's International Bank for Reconstruction and Development (IBRD) arm, and so is eligible for the HIPC initiative; a small number of countries whose debt-to-exports ratio is below 150 percent, but which qualify for HIPC on the basis of special criteria; all other HIPC-eligible countries, listed at idem, Debt Initiative for Heavily Indebted Poor Countries, Washington, DC, <www.worldbank.org/hipc>, viewed 24 October 2000; countries that are ineligible for the HIPC initiative because they are deemed creditworthy enough for the IBRD, but which meet the criteria in text; and Afghanistan and Indonesia, which are listed as "severely indebted low income" in idem, *Global Development Finance*, op. cit. note 3, pp. 143–44. On likelihood of repayment, see Daniel Cohen, *The HIPC Initiative: True and False Promises*, Working Paper (Paris: Organisation for Economic Co-operation and Development (OECD), Development Centre, 2000). Debt total excludes Afghanistan for lack of data, and is from World Bank, *Global Development Finance*, op. cit. note 4.

6. "Spend more" from U.N. Development Programme (UNDP), Management Development and Governance Division, *Debt and Sustainable Human Development*, Technical Advisory Paper No. 4 (New York: 1999), pp. 14–15; general decline in investment from Tony Killick, *Aid and the Political Economy of Policy Change* (London: Routledge, 1998), pp. 21–27; primary education and health spending from Carl Jayarajah, William Branson, and Binayak Sen, *Social Dimensions of Adjustment: World Bank Experience, 1980–93* (Washington, DC: World Bank, 1996), pp. 85–89; environmental protection from David Reed, "Conclusions: Short-term Environmental Impacts of Structural Adjustment Programs," in David Reed, ed., *Structural Adjustment, the Environment, and Sustainable Development* (London: Earthscan, 1996), p. 316.

7. Mexico from Joan M. Nelson, "The Politics of Pro-Poor Adjustment," in Joan M. Nelson, ed., *Fragile Coalitions: The Politics of Economic Adjustment* (Oxford: Transaction Books, 1989), p. 111; Wilfredo Cruz and Robert Repetto, *The Environmental Effects of Stabilization and Structural Adjustment Programs: The Philippines Case* (Washington, DC: World Resources Institute (WRI), 1992), p. 50; Brazil from Giovanni Andrea Cornia, "Economic Decline and Human Welfare in the First Half of the 1980s," in Giovanni Andrea Cornia, Richard Jolly, and Frances Stewart, eds., *Adjustment with a Human Face*, vol. 1 (Oxford: Clarendon Press, 1987), pp. 44–45.

8. World Bank, Debt Initiative for Heavily Indebted Poor Countries, op. cit. note 5; debt total from idem, *Global Development Finance*, op. cit. note 4; other write-offs from U.S. General Accounting Office (GAO), *Developing Countries: Debt Relief Initiative for Poor Countries Faces Challenges* (Washington, DC: U.S. Government Printing Office (GPO), 2000), p. 74; 45 percent and 55 percent are Worldwatch estimates, based on David Andrews et al., *Debt Relief for Low-Income Countries: The Enhanced HIPC Initiative*, Pamphlet Series No. 51 (Washington, DC: IMF, 2000), on World Bank, *Global Development Finance*, op. cit. note 3, pp. 144–46, on idem, *Global Development Finance*, op. cit. note 4, and on Horst Köhler and James D. Wolfensohn, "Debt Relief for the Poorest Countries: Milestone Achieved," joint statement, background charts, World Bank and IMF, Washington, DC, 22 December 2000, <wbln0018.worldbank.org/news/pressrelease.nsf/Attachments/hipccharts122200.pdf/$File/hipccharts122200.pdf>. Estimates assume all 41 eligible countries participate.

9. Benefits from Stephen Eccles and Catherine Gwin, *Supporting Effective Aid: A Framework for Future Concessional Funding of Multilateral Development Banks* (Washington, DC: Overseas Development Council (ODC), 1999), p. 13.

10. Robert Andrews, *The Columbia Dictionary of Quotations* (New York: Columbia University Press, 1993).

11. John Kenneth Galbraith, *A Short History of Financial Euphoria*, 2nd ed. (New York: Penguin Books, 1993), p. 13.

12. Donald D. Hester, "Bonds," in John Eatwell et al., eds., *The New Palgrave: A Dictionary of Economics*, vol. 1 (New York: Stockton Press Ltd., 1998), p. 261; Denise Schmandt-Besserat, "The Earliest Precursors of Writing," *Scientific American*, June 1978, pp. 50–59.

13. Wriston from Karin Lissakers, *Banks, Borrowers, and the Establishment: A Revisionist Account of the International Debt Crisis* (New York: BasicBooks, 1991), p. 182; A.G. Kenwood and A.L. Lougheed, *The Growth of the International Economy, 1820–1990: An Introductory Text*, 3rd ed. (London: Routledge, 1992), pp. 36–41.

14. Britannica.com, "Edward III," Chicago, viewed 23 September 2000; Saint-Simon from Bruce Rich, *Mortgaging the Earth: The World Bank, Environmental Impoverishment, and the Crisis of Development* (Boston: Beacon Press, 1994), pp. 215–20.

15. Uses of capital from Kenwood and Lougheed, op. cit. note 13, pp. 36–41; capital exports from Suter, op. cit. note 3, p. 49.

16. Profitability from Peter H. Lindert and Peter J. Morton, "How Sovereign Debt Has Worked," in Jeffrey D. Sachs, ed., *Developing Country Debt and the World Economy* (Chicago: University of Chicago Press, 1989), pp. 229–30.

17. Tulips and 1929 from Galbraith, op. cit. note 11, pp. 26–34, 70–86; Suter, op. cit. note 3, pp. 61–63. Figure 1 is based on ibid., pp. 70–71, and on Worldwatch estimates, based on World Bank, *Global Development Finance*, op. cit. note 3, pp. 158–71, on idem, *Annual Report* (Washington, DC: various years), notes to IBRD and IDA financial statements, and on IMF, *Annual Report* (Washington, DC: various years), notes to financial statements. Figure 1 includes defaults, consolidation periods (agreed periods during which no payments are made), and instances of countries going into "nonaccrual" status with the World Bank or "overdue" status with the IMF. Five defaults—Bulgaria's in 1932, China's in 1939, Czechoslovakia's in 1960, East Germany's in 1949, and Russia's in 1918—are treated as having terminated at the end of 1989, when the organization representing holders of these nations' bonds, the London-based Corporation of Foreign Bondholders, dissolved.

18. For a review of theories, see Suter, op. cit. note 3, pp. 33–41; market dynamics from Galbraith, op. cit. note 11, pp. 12–28; Great Britain from Suter, op. cit. note 3, p. 49.

19. Colombia from John H. Makin, *The Global Debt Crisis: America's Growing Involvement* (New York: Basic Books, 1983), p. 50.

20. S.C. Gwynne, "Adventures in the Loan Trade," *Harper's*, September 1983, p. 24.

21. Quote from Sampson, op. cit. note 2, p. 49; Britannica.com, "Bankruptcy," Chicago, viewed 23 September 2000; nine years from Suter, op. cit. note 3, p. 91.

22. Patricia Adams, *Odious Debts: Loose Lending, Corruption, and the Third World's Environmental Legacy* (London: Earthscan, 1991), pp. 162–70.

23. Frequent defaulters from Suter, op. cit. note 3, p. 69; statistics from Lindert and Morton, op. cit. note 16, p. 231; overlending from Sampson, op. cit. note 2, p. 35.

24. World Bank, *Global Development Finance*, op. cit. note 4. Figure 2 is based on ibid., is missing the short-term debt total for 1970, and, for lack of data, counts a relatively small amount of loans to private companies from the International Finance Corporation, the European Bank for Reconstruction and Development, and other official lenders as made by private lenders.

25. World Bank, *Global Development Finance*, op. cit. note 4.

26. Ibid.

27. Interest rates from U.S. Federal Reserve, Washington, DC, <www.federalreserve.gov/releases/H15/data/m/prime.txt>, viewed 19 August 2000; quote from Lissakers, op. cit. note 13, p. 84; on waste and export prices, see sources for later sections; debt from World Bank, op. cit. note 24.

28. Worldwatch estimates, based on World Bank, *Global Development Finance*, op. cit. note 4, and on idem, op. cit. note 24. Figures assume that 100 percent of net transfers on short-term debt each year were to private creditors. The true figures may be higher or lower. An analysis of data from the joint OECD-BIS-IMF-World Bank *Statistics on External Debt* database, which are not directly comparable to data from the World Bank's *Global Development Finance* database, suggests that 80–90 percent of the net transfers on short-term debt during 1983–98 were to or from private creditors.

29. Figure 4 has Worldwatch estimates based on World Bank, *Global Development Finance*, op. cit. note 4, and on idem, op. cit. note 24, and includes transactions with the IMF, but excludes those between official lenders, such as the IFC, and private borrowers, for lack of data. Low-income countries in a given year are those whose GNP per capita was $855 (in 1999 dollars) or less, following World Bank, *Annual Report*, op. cit. note 3, p. 141, and using the GNP per capita estimates computed with the "Atlas" method from idem, *World Development Indicators*, op. cit. note 4, and using the U.S. implicit GNP price deflator to convert to constant 1999 dollars. On tally of 47, see note 5.

30. Figures are Worldwatch estimates, based on World Bank, *Global Development Finance*, op. cit. note 4, and exclude Afghanistan for lack of data; Census Bureau, op. cit. note 4; Stockholm International Peace Research Institute (SIPRI), *SIPRI Yearbook 2000: Armaments, Disarmament and International Security* (Oxford: Oxford University Press, 2000), Table 5.1; John Garrett and Angela Travis, *Unfinished Business: The World's Leaders and the Millennium Debt Challenge* (London: Jubilee 2000 Coalition, 1999).

31. UNDP, *Human Development Report 2000* (New York: Oxford University Press, 2000), pp. 159–160, 268. Tally of 37 includes Afghanistan, Liberia, and Somalia, which the UNDP does not classify, for lack of some data, but which almost certainly are of "low human development." Zambia budget shares from idem, op. cit. note 6, pp. 14–15; other Zambia information from UNICEF, *Children in Jeopardy: The Challenge of Freeing Poor Nations from the Shackles of Debt* (New York: 1999), p. 11.

32. Debt prices from John Garrett, Senior Researcher, Jubilee 2000 Coalition, London, e-mail message to author, 15 August 2000; Worldwatch estimates, based on Cohen, op. cit. note 5. Note that about $60 billion of the "loss" arises because loans made on concessional terms have an intentional grant element.

33. Frances Moore Lappé, Joseph Collins, and Peter Rosset, *World Hunger: Twelve Myths*, 2nd ed. (New York: Grove Press, 1998), pp. 144–45.

34. World Bank, Debt Initiative for Heavily Indebted Poor Countries, op. cit. note 5; Cohen, op. cit. note 5. Note that about $44 billion of the "loss" arises because loans on concessional terms have an intentional grant element.

35. Worldwatch estimate, based on Transparency International (TI), "Transparency International Releases the Year 2000 Corruption Perceptions Index," press release (Berlin: 13 September 2000).

36. Capital flight from World Bank, *World Debt Tables 1992–93: External Finance for Developing Countries*, Vol. 1 (Washington, DC: 1992), p. 43; Duvalier from Lissakers, op. cit. note 13, pp. 146–47; Dieter Frisch, *Export Credit Insurance and the Fight against International Corruption*, TI Working Paper (Berlin: TI, 1999).

37. Rita Tullberg, "Military-Related Debt in Non-oil Developing Countries," in SIPRI, *SIPRI Yearbook 1985* (London: Taylor & Francis, 1985); Susan Willett, *The Arms Trade, Debt & Development* (London: Campaign Against Arms Trade, 1999); Bruce Rich, "Exporting Destruction," *Environmental Forum*, September/October 2000, p. 38.

38. Worldwatch estimates, based on Freedom House, *Annual Survey of Freedom Country Scores 1972–73 to 1999–2000* (Washington, DC: 2000).

39. Juan Antonio Morales and Jeffrey D. Sachs, "Bolivia's Economic Crisis," in Sachs, op. cit. note 16, pp. 57–65.

40. Brazil from Lissakers, op. cit. note 13, pp. 51, 66; Mahn-Je Kim, "The Republic of Korea's Successful Economic Development and the World Bank," in Devesh Kapur, John P. Lewis, and Richard Webb, eds., *The World Bank: Its First Half Century*, Vol. 2 (Washington, DC: Brookings Institution Press, 1997), pp. 22–26.

41. Catherine Caufield, *Masters of Illusion: The World Bank and the Poverty of Nations* (New York: Henry Holt and Company, 1996), pp. 70–87; Mozambique from George, op. cit. note 2, pp. 86–87; Tanzania from World Bank, *Assessing Aid: What Works, What Doesn't, and Why* (Oxford: Oxford University Press, 1998), p. 1; figures are for projects whose last loan disbursement occurred during the 1990s, and are from Nagy Hanna et al., *1999 Annual Review of Development Effectiveness* (Washington, DC: World Bank, Operations Evaluation Department (OED), 1999), p. 43.

42. Christopher Barr, *Banking on Sustainability: A Critical Assessment of Structural Adjustment in Indonesia's Forest and Estate Crop Industries* (Bogor and Washington, DC: Center for International Forestry Research and World Wide Fund For Nature (WWF), forthcoming).

43. James P. Grant, *The State of the World's Children 1989* (Oxford, UK: Oxford University Press, 1989), pp. 30–31.

44. Dani Rodrik, *The New Global Economy and Developing Countries: Making Openness Work*, Policy Essay No. 24 (Washington, DC: ODC, 1999), pp. 68–77.

45. United front from Suter, op. cit. note 3, p. 106; "smaller" is a Worldwatch estimate, based on World Bank, op. cit. note 24.

46. Worldwatch updates of Angus Maddison, *Monitoring the World Economy, 1820–1992* (Paris: OECD, 1995), pp. 21–22, using deflators and recent growth rates from IMF, *World Economic Outlook*, electronic database, Washington, DC, September 2000, and population data from Census Bureau, op. cit. note 4; Daniel Cohen, *Growth and External Debt: A New Perspective on the African and Latin American Tragedies*, Paper No. 9715 (Paris: Ecole Normale Supérieure, Centre d'Etudes Prospectives d'Economie Mathématique Appliquées à la Planification, July 1997), pp. 11–15.

47. General decline in investment from Killick, op. cit. note 6, pp. 21–27; decline in primary education and health spending from Jayarajah, Branson, and Sen, op. cit. note 6, pp. 85–89.

48. Thailand from George, op. cit. note 2, p. 61; terms of trade from IMF, *International Financial Statistics Yearbook 2000* (Washington, DC: 2000), pp. 144–45; trade barriers from Nicholas Stern, Chief Economist, World Bank, press conference to launch *Global Economic Prospects and the Developing Countries 2001*, World Bank, Washington, DC, 5 December 2000, <www.worldbank.org/prospects/gep2001/pressconf.htm>, and from World Bank, *Global Economic Prospects and the Developing Countries 2001* (Washington, DC: 2000), pp. 17–23.

49. Mixed effects on poor from Tony Killick, "Structural Adjustment and Poverty Alleviation: An Interpretive Survey," *Development and Change*, vol. 26 (1995), p. 309; influence of middle class and civil servants from Arthur MacEwan, "Latin America: Why Not Repudiate?" *Monthly Review*, September 1986, pp. 1–13.

50. World Bank study is Jayarajah, Branson, and Sen, op. cit. note 6, pp. 85–89; George, op. cit. note 2, pp. 100–05, 111.

51. UNICEF from Grant, op. cit. note 43, p. 1; Brazil from Cornia, Jolly, and Stewart, op. cit. note 7, pp. 43–45.

52. Debt role in recession from Manuel Pastor, Jr., "The Effects of IMF Programs in the Third World: Debate and Evidence from Latin America," *World Development*, vol. 15, no. 2 (1987), pp. 249–62; Jamaica from George, op. cit. note 2, pp. 179–80; Mexico from Nelson, op. cit. note 7, p. 111; Merih Celâsun and Dani Rodrik, "Turkish Experience with Debt: Macroeconomic Policy and Performance," in Sachs, op. cit. note 16, pp. 201–05; Stanley Fischer, "Resolving the International Debt Crisis," in Sachs, op. cit. note 16, p. 314.

53. Cruz and Repetto, op. cit. note 7, p. 50; Venezuela from Reed, op. cit. note 6, p. 323.

54. Reed, op. cit. note 6, p. 316.

55. James Kahn and Judith McDonald, "International Debt and Deforestation," in Katrina Brown and David W. Pearce, eds., *The Causes of Tropical Deforestation: The Economic and Statistical Analysis of Factors Giving Rise to the Loss of the Tropical Forests* (Vancouver, BC: UBC Press, 1994), pp. 57–67. See also Ana Doris Capistrano, "Tropical Forest Depletion and the Changing Macroeconomy, 1968–85," in Brown and Pearce, eds., op. cit. this note, pp. 68–85, which finds less significance for debt burden, but controls for currency devaluation events, which are closely tied to adjustment stress and emerge as a statistically significant predictor of deforestation. Tanzania from Reed, op. cit. note 6, p. 307.

56. Killick, op. cit. note 6, pp. 21–27.

57. Robert Wade, "Selective Industrial Policies in East Asia: Is *The East Asian Miracle* Right?" in Albert Fishlow et al., *Miracle or Design? Lessons from the East Asian Experience*, Policy Essay No. 11 (Washington, DC: ODC, 1994), p. 59; Rodrik, op. cit. note 44, pp. 1–4.

58. Ibid., pp. 77–100, 150.

59. Killick, op. cit. note 6, pp. 100–27, endpapers.

60. Zambia from ibid., pp. 112–13; Bolivia from Ramani Gunatilaka and Ana Marr, "Conditionality and Adjustment in South-east Asia and Latin America," in ibid., pp. 74–78; Jane Harrigan, "Malawi," in Paul Mosley, Jane Harrigan, and John Toye, *Aid and Power: The World Bank and Policy-Based Lending*, vol. 2 (London: Routledge, 1991), pp. 223–34.

61. Shantayanan Devarajan, David Dollar, and Torgny Holmgren, *Aid and Reform in Africa: Lessons from Ten Case Studies* (Washington, DC: World Bank, forthcoming), <www.worldbank.org/research/aid/africa/intro.htm>; Carol Lancaster, "The World Bank in Africa since 1980: The Politics of Structural Adjustment Lending," in Kapur, Lewis, and Webb, op. cit. note 40, p. 171.

62. Harry S. Truman, inaugural address, 20 January 1949, available at the Whistlestop Project, Independence, MO, <www.whistlestop.org>.

63. *The American Heritage Dictionary of the English Language*, 4th ed. (New York: Bartleby.com, 2000).

64. Lissakers, op. cit. note 13, pp. 18–45.

65. Sampson, op. cit. note 2, p. 12.

66. Worldwatch estimates, based on World Bank, *Global Development Finance*, op. cit. note 4, and on idem, op. cit. note 24. Figures exclude Afghanistan for lack of data.

67. Truman, op. cit. note 62.

68. Graham Hancock, *Lords of Poverty: The Power, Prestige, and Corruption of the International Aid Business* (New York: Atlantic Monthly Press, 1989), pp. 176–81; "billion-dollar debtors" from World Bank, op. cit. note 24.

69. Business coalition from Caufield, op. cit. note 41, p. 317; quote from Adams, op. cit. note 22, p. 87; ECA role in nuclear exports from Rich, op. cit. note 37, pp. 36–38; "uncompetitive" from Christopher Flavin and Nicholas Lenssen, *Power Surge: Guide to the Coming Energy Revolution* (New York: W.W. Norton and Company, 1994), p. 251.

70. Adams, op. cit. note 22, p. 88.

71. World Bank, *Annual Report*, op. cit. note 3, p. 29; "unlikely" from Caufield, op. cit. note 41, p. 325.

72. Truman, op. cit. note 62.

73. Alex Duncan, "The World Bank as a Project Lender: Experience from Eastern Africa," in Kapur, Lewis, and Webb, op. cit. note 40, pp. 385–429; Devarajan, Dollar, and Holmgren, op. cit. note 61. Most development loans to the poorest nations are made on concessional terms, with interest rates as low as 0.5 percent per annum. Whether the borrower is judged to bear most of the cost of whatever such loans finance depends on the choice of discount rate. The conventional choice is a commercial interest rate, perhaps 7 percent, which makes sense if the lower interest charges on concessional loans free up money that borrowing governments can invest, and if governments actually invest all the savings in ways that generate a commercial rate of return over the 40–50-year life of the loan. In the poorest countries, where these assumptions seem questionable, a social discount rate of, say, 3 percent, seems more meaningful. With a lower discount rate, the borrower bears most of the cost of whatever is financed. That is, the "grant element" of the loan is well below 50 percent.

74. McNamara from Devesh Kapur, John P. Lewis, and Richard Webb, eds., *The World Bank: Its First Half Century*, vol. 1 (Washington, DC: Brookings Institution Press, 1997), p. 692; World Bank, "Effective Implementation: Key to Development Impact," Working Paper R92-195 (Washington, DC: 1992), p. iii; quote from Robert Wade, *Unpacking the World Bank: Lending versus Leverage*, unpublished paper, Washington, DC, March 1989, cited in Paul Mosley, Jane Harrigan, and John Toye, *Aid and Power: The World Bank and Policy-Based Lending*, vol. 1 (London: Routledge, 1991), p. 72; Garrett and Travis, op. cit. note 30.

75. Role of debt trouble from World Bank, op. cit. note 41, p. 41; Paul Collier, "Learning from Failure: The International Financial Institutions as Agencies of Restraint in Africa," in Andreas Schedler et al., eds., *The Self-Restraining State* (Boulder, CO: Lynn Rienner, 1999), p. 321.

76. Walden Bello, "ADB 2000: Senior Officials and Internal Documents Paint Institution in Confusion," in Focus on the Global South, *Creating Poverty: The ADB in Asia* (Bangkok: 2000), p. 9; 1997 report from Bruce Rich, "The Smile on a Child's Face: From the Culture of Loan Approval to the Culture of Development Effectiveness? The World Bank under James Wolfensohn," (forthcoming); Robert Wade, "Greening the Bank: The Struggle over the Environment," in Kapur, Lewis, and Webb, op. cit. note 40, p. 731; retired World Bank employee, interview with author, 26 January 2001.

77. Caufield, op. cit. note 41, pp. 207–08; International Rivers Network, "Guatemalan Massacre Survivor Demands Reparations from the World Bank and the Inter-American Development Bank," press release (Berkeley, CA: 10 April 2000); total debt from World Bank, *Global Development Finance*, op. cit. note 4.

78. Table 3 is from the following: Bolivia and Argentina from Gunatilaka and Marr, op. cit. note 60, pp. 74–78, and from Morales and Sachs, op. cit.

note 39, pp. 73–77; Zambia from Killick, op. cit. note 6, pp. 112–13; Malawi from Harrigan, op. cit. note 60, pp. 223–34; Philippines from Paul Mosley, "The Philippines," in Mosley, Harrigan, and Toye, op. cit. note 60, pp. 44–54, and from Killick, op. cit. note 6, p. 104; Kenya from Collier, op. cit. note 75, p. 321; sub-Saharan Africa from Devesh Kapur and Richard Webb, *Governance-Related Conditionalities of the International Finance Institutions*, G–24 Discussion series, N. 6 (Cambridge, MA: Harvard University, Center for International Development, 2000) p. 6; typical compliance from Mosley, Harrigan, and Toye, op. cit. note 74, pp. 134–36; Colin Kirkpatrick and Ziya Onis, "Turkey," in idem, op. cit. note 60, pp. 23–24, 30.

79. World Bank from Mosley, Harrigan, and Toye, op. cit. note 74, p. 166, for the 1980s, and from Killick, op. cit. note 6, p. 30, for the early 1990s; IMF from idem, *IMF Programmes in Developing Countries: Design and Impact* (London: Routledge, 1995), pp. 61–63, 118–19.

80. Navroz K. Dubash and Colin Filer, "Papua New Guinea," in Frances J. Seymour and Navroz K. Dubash, *The Right Conditions: The World Bank, Structural Adjustment, and Forest Policy Reform* (Washington, DC: WRI, 2000), pp. 35–46; "rare" from Frances Seymour, WRI, presentation given at "IMF and World Bank Accountability: Closing the Gap between Rhetoric and Reality," conference sponsored by Globalization Challenge Institute, Washington, DC, 9 June 2000.

81. Lissakers, op. cit. note 13, p. 227.

82. Net transfers from World Bank, *Global Development Finance*, op. cit. note 4; sources for figures in text and Figure 6 are those for Figure 1.

83. Bolivia from Jeremy Bulow and Kenneth Rogoff, "Cleaning Up Third World Debt without Getting Taken to the Cleaners," *Journal of Economic Perspectives*, winter 1990, p. 33. Other swaps from World Bank, op. cit. note 36, pp. 52–53, 93.

84. Melissa Moye, *Overview of Debt Conversion* (London: Debt Relief International, 2000), p. 14.

85. Totals from Ricardo Bayon, independent consultant, New York, unpublished tabulation, e-mail message to author, 7 July 2000; debt-for-development swaps from Moye, op. cit. note 84, pp. 12–15.

86. Brady from Lissakers, op. cit. note 13, pp. 227–28; plan from World Bank, op. cit. note 36, pp. 52–54.

87. World Bank, op. cit. note 36, pp. 52–54.

88. Idem, *Global Development Finance*, op. cit. note 3, pp. 158–62.

89. Idem, op. cit. note 36, p. 75; indicators from idem, *Global Development*

Finance, op. cit. note 3, pp. 169–71.

90. Suter, op. cit. note 3, p. 99.

91. Jubilee 2000 Coalition, "Who We Are," London, <www.jubilee2000 uk.org/main.html>, viewed 23 August 2000; idem, "Italian Government Break with Other G8 Creditors on Third World Debt Cancellation," press release (London: 13 July 2000); Leviticus 25–28, New English Bible.

92. Program details from Andrews et al., op. cit. note 8; 45 percent is a Worldwatch estimate, based on ibid., on World Bank, *Global Development Finance,* op. cit. note 3, pp. 144–46, and on idem, *Global Development Finance,* op. cit. note 4, and assuming that all 41 eligible countries participate.

93. GAO, op. cit. note 8, p. 74; 55 percent is a Worldwatch estimate, based on Andrews et al., op. cit. note 8, on World Bank, *Global Development Finance,* op. cit. note 3, pp. 144–46, on idem, *Global Development Finance,* op. cit. note 4, and on Köhler and Wolfensohn, op. cit. note 8.

94. Adam Smith, *An Inquiry into the Nature and Causes of the Wealth of Nations* (New York: P.F. Collier & Son, 1902), Book 5, Chapter III, p. 376.

95. The World Bank considers the four countries creditworthy enough to receive loans from its IBRD lending arm, and IBRD-eligible countries cannot enter the HIPC program. Standard & Poors, "Sovereign Ratings List," 19 January 2001, <www.standardandpoors.com/ratings/sovereigns/ ratingslist.htm>. Moody's Investors Services, "Ratings List: Government Bonds & Country Ceilings," 16 January 2001, <www.moodys.com/moodys/ cust/RatingAction/rList.asp?busLineId=7>. Other exclusions from Jacob Kolster, HIPC Implementation Unit, World Bank, Washington, DC, e-mail to author, 1 February 2001.

96. "Arbitrary" and figure of 15–20 percent from European Network on Debt and Development (EURODAD), "Rethinking HIPC Debt Sustainability," Eurodad Background Paper, Brussels, July 2000; Germany from Joseph Hanlon, *Debt, Default and Relief in the Past: And How We Are Demanding That the Poor Pay More This Time* (London: Jubilee 2000 Coalition, 1998).

97. Figure of 31 percent is expressed relative to the present value of HIPC debt, estimated at $161 billion, not the face value of $205 billion, and is a Worldwatch estimate, based on techniques in Cohen, op. cit. note 5. According to these techniques, about 10 percent of the reduction in present value of debt of the Worldwatch 47 will reach the debtors through lower net transfers to creditors.

98. Debt reduction from Köhler and Wolfensohn, op. cit. note 8; debt service reduction from Jamie Drummond, Drop the Debt, London, e-mail to author, 15 January 2001.

99. Uganda from GAO, op. cit. note 8, p. 65; EURODAD, "Panel on PRS: Some Cross-Country Lessons So Far," presented at World Bank executive directors' meeting, Washington, DC, 4 December 2000.

100. EURODAD, *Poverty Reduction Strategies: What Have We Learned So Far?* (draft) (Brussels: 23 September 2000).

101. Joan M. Nelson, Senior Associate, ODC, interview with author, 17 May 2000; GAO, op. cit. note 8, pp. 123–27.

102. Irûngûh Houghton, Manager, Policy Research Unit, ActionAid Kenya, Nairobi, interview with author, 15 June 2000; on the difficulty of enforcing governance-related conditions, see Kapur and Webb, op. cit. note 78; Ghana and Uganda from GAO, op. cit. note 8, p. 57.

103. GAO, op. cit. note 8, p. 57.

104. World Bank, Debt Initiative for Heavily Indebted Poor Countries, op. cit. note 5; Honduras and Burkina Faso from EURODAD, op. cit. note 100.

105. Face value of debts from World Bank, *Global Development Finance*, op. cit. note 4; "market" values are Worldwatch estimates, based on techniques in Cohen, op. cit. note 5; U.S. Office of Management and Budget, *Budget of the United States Government, Fiscal Year 2001* (Washington, DC: GPO, 2000), p. 285; SIPRI, op. cit. note 30, Table 5.1.

106. John Maynard Keynes, *The Economic Consequences of the Peace* (London: Macmillan and Co., Ltd., 1919), pp. 209–10, cited in Vincent Ferraro and Melissa Rosser, "Global Debt and Third World Development," in Michael Klare and Daniel Thomas, eds., *World Security: Challenges for a New Century* (New York: St. Martin's Press, 1994), pp. 332–55.

107. Robert L. Heilbroner, *The Worldly Philosophers: The Lives, Times, and Ideas of Great Economic Thinkers*, rev. ed. (New York: Simon and Schuster, 1961), pp. 223–25.

108. GAO, op. cit. note 8, pp. 72, 74.

109. Figure 7 is from Adam Lerrick, "The Initiative Is Lacking," *Euromoney*, September 2000, and uses present value rather than face value for debt figures.

110. 1998 debt from World Bank, *Global Development Finance*, op. cit. note 3, p. 146; GAO, op. cit. note 8, pp. 42–56. Debt figures are in present value terms.

111. Subsidies figure is from OECD, *Agricultural Policies in OECD Countries* (Paris: 2000), p. 161, and is for the "OECD 24," which excludes new OECD members such as Mexico and Poland; Uruguay Round from Kevin Watkins and Michael Windfuhr, "Agriculture in the Uruguay Round: Implications for

Sustainable Development in Developing Countries," WWF International Discussion Paper (Gland, Switzerland: WWF, 1995), p. 16; textiles from Biplab Dasgupta, *Structural Adjustment, Global Trade and the New Political Economy of Development* (London: Zed Books, 1998), p 156–58; Camdessus from GAO, op. cit. note 8, p. 35.

112. U.S. Department of Commerce, Office of Africa, "Africa Growth and Opportunity Act," Washington, DC, <www.agoa.gov>, viewed 2 February 2001; Jim Fisher-Thompson and Jody Hamilton, "AGOA to Mark Shift in the Way Americans View Africa," U.S. Department of State, International Information Programs, Washington, DC, <www.usinfo.state.gov/regional/af/trade/a0101801.htm>, viewed 2 February 2001.

113. Rich, op. cit. note 37, p. 39; long-term trend from Kenwood and Lougheed, op. cit. note 13, p. 284.

114. Rodolfo A. Bulatao, *The Value of Family Planning Programs in Developing Countries* (Santa Monica, CA: RAND, 1998), pp. iv–viii.

115. Jubilee 2000 Coalition, "Malawi Rejects World Bank AIDS Loan Because of Existing Debt Burden," London, <www.jubilee2000uk.org>, viewed 11 February 2001.

116. Bilateral agencies from Joseph Hanlon, *Details and Interpretation of the Köln Debt Initiative* (London: Jubilee 2000 Coalition, 1999).

117. World Bank, OED, *Higher Impact Adjustment Lending: Initial Evaluation,* vol. 1 (Washington, DC: 1999), p. i; "probably put to better use" based on World Bank, op. cit. note 41, pp. 34–40.

118. OED from Catherine Gwin, "U.S. Relationship with the World Bank, 1945–1992," in Kapur, Lewis, and Webb, op. cit. note 40, pp. 267–68.

119. Kunibert Raffer, "What's Good for the United States Must Be Good for the World: Advocating an International Chapter 9 Insolvency," in Camilla Nielsen et al., eds., *From Cancún to Vienna: International Development in a New World* (Vienna: Bruno Kreisky Forum for International Dialogue, 1993), pp. 64–74; Adams, op. cit. note 22, pp. 162–70.

Worldwatch Papers

No. of Copies

Worldwatch Papers by David Malin Roodman

_____WWP0155 Still Waiting for the Jubilee: Pragmatic Solutions for the Third World Debt Crisis

_____WWP0134 Getting the Signals Right: Tax Reform to Protect the Environment and the Economy

_____WWP0133 Paying the Piper: Subsidies, Politics, and the Environment

_____WWP0124 A Building Revolution: How Ecology and Health Concerns Are Transforming Construction _(with Nicholas Lenssen)_

Climate Change, Energy, and Materials

_____WWP0151 Micropower: The Next Electrical Era

_____WWP0149 Paper Cuts: Recovering the Paper Landscape

_____WWP0144 Mind Over Matter: Recasting the Role of Materials in Our Lives

_____WWP0138 Rising Sun, Gathering Winds: Policies to Stabilize the Climate and Strengthen Economies

_____WWP0130 Climate of Hope: New Strategies for Stabilizing the World's Atmosphere

Ecological and Human Health

_____WWP0153 Why Poison Ourselves? A Precautionary Approach to Synthetic Chemicals

_____WWP0148 Nature's Cornucopia: Our Stake in Plant Diversity

_____WWP0145 Safeguarding The Health of Oceans

_____WWP0142 Rocking the Boat: Conserving Fisheries and Protecting Jobs

_____WWP0141 Losing Strands in the Web of Life: Vertebrate Declines and the Conservation of Biological Diversity

_____WWP0140 Taking a Stand: Cultivating a New Relationship with the World's Forests

_____WWP0129 Infecting Ourselves: How Environmental and Social Disruptions Trigger Disease

_____WWP0128 Imperiled Waters, Impoverished Future: The Decline of Freshwater Ecosystems

Economics, Institutions, and Security

_____WWP0152 Working for the Environment: A Growing Source of Jobs

_____WWP0146 Ending Violent Conflict

_____WWP0139 Investing in the Future: Harnessing Private Capital Flows for Environmentally Sustainable Development

_____WWP0137 Small Arms, Big Impact: The Next Challenge of Disarmament

_____WWP0127 Eco-Justice: Linking Human Rights and the Environment

_____WWP0126 Partnership for the Planet: An Environmental Agenda for the United Nations

_____WWP0125 The Hour of Departure: Forces That Create Refugees and Migrants

_____WWP0122 Budgeting for Disarmament: The Costs of War and Peace

Food, Water, Population, and Urbanization

_____WWP0150 Underfed and Overfed: The Global Epidemic of Malnutrition

_____WWP0147 Reinventing Cities for People and the Planet

_____WWP0143 Beyond Malthus: Sixteen Dimensions of the Population Problem

_____WWP0136 The Agricultural Link: How Environmental Deterioration Could Disrupt Economic Progress

_____WWP0135 Recycling Organic Waste: From Urban Pollutant to Farm Resource

_____WWP0132 Dividing the Waters: Food Security, Ecosystem Health, and the New Politics of Scarcity

_____WWP0131 Shrinking Fields: Cropland Loss in a World of Eight Billion

_____Total copies (transfer number to order form on next page)

PUBLICATION ORDER FORM

NOTE: Many Worldwatch publications can be downloaded as PDF files from our website at **www.worldwatch.org**. Orders for printed publications can also be placed on the web.

_____ *State of the World:* **$15.95**
The annual book used by journalists, activists, scholars, and policymakers worldwide to get a clear picture of the environmental problems we face.

_____ **State of the World Library: $30.00 (international subscribers $45)**
Receive *State of the World* and all Worldwatch Papers as they are released during the calendar year.

_____ *Vital Signs:* **$13.95**
The book of trends that are shaping our future in easy-to-read graph and table format, with a brief commentary on each trend.

_____ **WORLD WATCH magazine subscription: $20.00 (international subscribers $35.00)**
Stay abreast of global environmental trends and issues with our award-winning, eminently readable bimonthly magazine.

_____ **Worldwatch CD-ROM: $89.00**
Contains global agricultural, energy, economic, environmental, social, and military indicators from all current Worldwatch publications. Includes *Vital Signs* and *State of the World* as they are published. CD contains Microsoft Excel spreadsheets 5.0/95 (*.xls) for Windows, and works on both Mac and PC.

_____ **Worldwatch Papers—See list on previous page Single copy: $5.00**
any combination of titles: 2–5: $4.00 ea. • 6–20: $3.00 ea. • 21 or more: $2.00 ea.

$4.00* Shipping and Handling *($8.00 outside North America)*
minimum charge for S&H; call (800) 555-2028 for bulk order S&H

_____ **TOTAL** (U.S. dollars only)

Make check payable to: Worldwatch Institute, P.O. Box 879 Oxon Hill, MD 20797 USA

❑ Enclosed is my check or purchase order for U.S. $_____

❑ AMEX ❑ VISA ❑ MasterCard _____
Card Number   Expiration Date

signature

name   **daytime phone #**

address

city   **state**   **zip/country**

**phone: (800) 555-2028   fax: (301) 567-9553   e-mail: wwpub@worldwatch.org
website: www.worldwatch.org**

Wish to make a tax-deductible contribution? Contact Worldwatch to find out how your donation can help advance our work.